Appetizers

Mable & Gar Hoffman

Appetizers

Contents

Food Stylist: Mable Hoffman
Photography: deGennaro Associates

Published by HPBooks, a division of Price Stern Sloan, Inc.
360 North La Cienega Blvd., Los Angeles, CA 90048
ISBN 0-89586-711-7
Library of Congress Catalog Card No. 80-84672
©1980, 1988 HPBooks   Printed in U.S.A.
1st Printing, Revised Edition

Cover photo, clockwise starting at top right: Cheese Sticks, page 133; Salmon-Stuffed Tomatoes, page 69; Marinated Vegetables, page 61; Chicken Wing Drumsticks, page 53; Stuffed New Potatoes, page 147; Indonesian Pork Sate, page 20 and Treasure Island Shrimp, page 156.

Mable Hoffman's favorite subject is appetizers. Mable and her husband Gar have traveled widely studying the foods of other countries. Arriving at home, they search California markets for taste-alike foods and then develop recipes following authentic cuisines. They have enjoyed creating new and exciting appetizers and adding interest and zest to traditional pâtés, sandwiches and fondues for their own entertaining and now share these ideas with you.

Mable has authored several HPBooks publications including *Crockery Cookery, Crepe Cookery, Deep-Fry Cookery, Chocolate Cookery* and *Ice Cream.* Both *Crockery Cookery* and *Crepe Cookery* have won the R. T. French Tastemaker Award, the "Oscar" for cookbooks, as the best softcover cookbooks of the year.

Besides developing recipes for her own books, this professional Home Economist creates savory and delightful dishes for many commercial food firms. She does much of the food styling for HPBooks. She and her husband own and manage Hoffman Food Consultants.

Appetizer Cookery

According to historians, Western European hostesses fed weary travelers small portions of food to satisfy their hunger while they waited for the main meal. Then as now, appetizers served before a meal were not intended to take the place of dinner or be so filling the meal was not appreciated. Hostesses worried about what tidbits to serve and whether their guests would enjoy their efforts. Today, hostesses still worry as they serve appetizers to stimulate conversation or to put guests at ease as a pleasant evening begins or draws to a close. Hostesses have always needed a book which included easy to prepare or elegant appetizers and guidelines on how to combine a variety of appetizers at a single function. On page 10 we have suggested combinations of molds, pâtés, meat morsels, vegetable appetizers and many others you can use with confidence as you entertain guests.

With little more than a snap of your fingers you can prepare some of the appetizers in this book and have them ready to serve. Others can be prepared and frozen weeks before, then are ready to serve as soon as thawed. Food has universal appeal and is often the ice-breaker at a cocktail party or open-house. Introduce a savory dip, fondue or small pieces of meat or fish and watch your party come alive. Imagine the pleasure of guests as they crowd around strategically arranged appetizers and conversation begins to flow.

In each chapter, you'll find traditional as well as new or up-dated versions of classic foods which fit today's way of life. We have included both hot and cold appetizers for family get-togethers as well as special parties or holidays. Most are finger foods to be eaten at parties or while sitting around the coffee table with friends. *Starters* are an exception. Starter appetizers are usually eaten at the table before dinner is served. They add an air of elegance to formal or special-event dinners.

PREPARING & STORING APPETIZERS

Most appetizers can be prepared without special equipment. However, if you have appliances, let them do the work and shorten your preparation time. We used an electric blender and a food processor to chop, puree and blend ingredients in many recipes. If you don't have these appliances, use a food grinder for firm foods or an electric mixer for soft foods. You may use a knife for finely mincing some ingredients, but you won't be able to get a smooth texture. Use your toaster oven to heat small bite-size pieces of meat, cheese or pastry. An electric deep-fryer with automatic control takes the guesswork out of making crispy fried tidbits. Because they don't require watching, slow cookers are handy for long cooking of meat to be chopped or shredded and to keep meatballs warm.

When foods must be heated at the last moment, microwave ovens heat appetizers in a very few minutes. Maintain ideal serving temperatures by holding appetizers on electric hot trays and in chafing dishes. Fondue pots, warming trays and chafing dishes are all invaluable for use at the serving table. If you don't have any of these, serve hot foods in casserole dishes that hold heat for a relatively long time.

Fancy molds make foods look pretty, but small bowls can be used as molds. Be sure to add attractive garnish to any molded foods. Cookie cutters in various shapes give you interesting and fancy party sandwiches or pastry decorations. Small tart pans or miniature muffin pans are just the right size for making appetizer tarts.

With adequate preplanning, you can do most preparations by yourself. Plan only one or two hot appetizers which must be prepared ahead and heated at the last minute. The remainder of your menu should include cold appetizers you can prepare ahead and serve without any last-minute attention.

To prevent moisture from penetrating, generously spread softened butter, margarine or cream cheese over bread before adding a filling. You'll need about 1/4 pound butter, margarine or cream cheese for each one-pound loaf of bread when making sandwiches, canapés or hors d'oeuvres. Let the spread soften at room temperature for ease in spreading. Avoid using melted butter or margarine as it soaks into the bread rather than coating the surface.

Purchase uncut loaves of sandwich bread for making sandwiches. Many bakeries will cut the bread lengthwise for you. Or you can cut your own. For ease in cutting, place loaves in the freezer about 30 minutes. This is long enough for the network of the bread to be set but not long enough for it to be frozen hard. Day-old bread is easier to cut and holds its shape better than fresh bread.

Hot appetizers should be served immediately after they are prepared; however, many must be given time for flavors to develop. Some dips and spreads can be stored in the refrigerator two to three days before they are needed. Bring them to room temperature before serving. Store all appetizers in tightly covered containers to prevent drying and use them within three to five days. If you plan to store them longer and their ingredients can be frozen, package them in airtight containers and place them in the freezer. For best quality, use frozen appetizers within three months. Thaw only the amount you anticipate using at one time. Never thaw and refreeze appetizers.

Do not freeze lettuce. Unless used in very small amounts, do not freeze celery, radishes, cucumbers or tomatoes, whole or chopped egg whites, mayonnaise or salad dressing, gelatins or aspics. Egg yolks, meats, fish and poultry freeze well. Butter or margarine and cream cheese are spreads that freeze without any problems.

Because breads freeze well, party sandwiches are ideal for freezing if the filling ingredients can be frozen. Freeze baked pastry shells and toast cups separately from their fillings. If they become too soft after thawing, preheat the oven to 350°F (175°C) and bake the shells 10 to 15 minutes before adding the filling.

Freeze appetizers in a single layer on a flat metal tray or baking sheet. If the appetizer must be stacked, place two pieces of waxed paper between layers, then package them in an airtight freezer container and store them in your freezer. Use only moisture-vapor-proof freezer bags or freezer wrap. Glass or plastic containers with air-tight seals are also acceptable. This is especially true when storing in frost-free freezers. The same process which removes moisture from the freezer removes moisture from food in improperly sealed packages.

SELECTING & SERVING APPETIZERS

Seldom are guests entertained where food is not offered. Whether it's at a mid-morning coffee, an afternoon tea, a reception, an open house, a friendly visit before and after the theater or game—any event is a legitimate time for serving appetizers.

Some appetizers are relatively inexpensive and can help you entertain without creating havoc with your budget. Others are quite expensive. Spreads using hard-cooked eggs or cottage cheese as a base go a long way and cost very little. Meat, shrimp, crab and caviar ingredients increase the cost of an appetizer, but flavor and elegance are worth the extra expense. We have designed a Guide for Special Events, page 10, with appetizer suggestions to meet anyone's budget or menu needs. Complete low-cost suggestions include a Twelve-Year-Old's Birthday, a Graduation Party and Budget Entertaining.

Select flavors and foods which will appeal to your guests. If you don't know their preferences, choose mild-flavored appetizers. For those who like the new and exciting, prepare your most creative dishes or some of those exotic-sounding recipes you've been wanting to try. Appetizer flavors should differ from main meal dishes. Curry-flavored appetizers will not enhance a meal flavored with curry. However, coordinate your appetizers with your dinner. When serving an ethnic dinner, start your party with appetizers from the same ethnic cuisine.

The number of appetizers you'll prepare for each person is influenced by several factors. Consider the variety of appetizers to be served, whether your guests are on diets and time span between when guests will arrive and when or if dinner will be served. As a general rule, plan five or six appetizers per guest. If your guests have had no lunch, they may partake heavily and you'll have to rush out to the kitchen to extend your supply. Then again, if guests are counting every calorie, you may have leftovers.

When entertaining two or three people before an early dinner you'll want one or two different appetizers. Consider serving one dip or spread and one pastry or hot puff. If your party will last several hours, serve a variety of appetizers including hearty ones such as meat balls, kabobs and some made with pastry or bread. For an open house or an anniversary celebration, we suggest a small buffet with four to six different kinds of appetizers arranged on several trays or plates.

For a party, plan your appetizer table with a center of interest. This can be a centerpiece of flowers or an elegant appetizer such as Caviar-Crowned Mold, page 99. When an appetizer centerpiece is used, have a replacement to use later. If a beverage is served, place it and silverware at the opposite end of the table from the plates. Be-

cause most appetizers are finger foods, have small plates, cocktail forks, wooden picks or wooden skewers available for guests to serve themselves. Keep everything relative in size. If appetizers are small, plates should be small. If food is large or will spread out, be sure the plate will accommodate it. If a cup or glass and appetizers will be on the same plate, the plate must be large enough for both.

Your buffet table can be placed against the wall so guests proceed from one end to the other. Or move it away from the wall so guests can approach from either end or move around the table clockwise. People generally start at the end where plates are stacked. If you are entertaining a very large group, have more than one table.

Visualize how appetizer trays will look as they are emptied. Large trays are difficult to keep filled and attractive-looking. It may be wiser to arrange your creations on several plates which can easily be replaced with full ones. Even though you prepare the appetizers by yourself, you may want someone to assist with serving and to keep appetizer trays filled.

Never crowd appetizers on a tray or plate. Guests should be able to remove one appetizer without touching any other. Arrange open-face sandwiches in a single layer on plates or small trays. Other sandwiches such as ribbons and pinwheels may be slightly overlapped or stacked in a neat arrangement. Cover and refrigerate additional plates of sandwiches and use to replace empty trays. Garnish trays with watercress, parsley, endive, cherry tomatoes or whole radishes. Place trays, bowls or serving pieces on your buffet table far enough apart so guests can set their plates down to serve themselves. It is best to use service pieces such as spoons or tongs that require only one hand to lift food.

Guide for Special Events

Success or failure of a party often depends on the right choice of foods to serve. Listed below are some appetizers appropriate for special events. **This is not a list of menus,** but a guide to be chosen from to fit an event or theme. Add to or subtract from the list to meet your own needs.

Father's Day Celebration
Pickled Eggs & Beets, page 38
Teriyaki Roll-Ups, page 19
Bacon & Cheese Deviled Eggs, page 40
Hot Crab Dip, page 48
Crab & Swiss on Sourdough, page 49
Bacon & Avocado Dip, page 116
Miniature Reubens, page 144
Shrimp Cocktail, page 147

Graduation Party
Mushroom-Burger Bites, page 20
Layered French Loaf, page 37
Chicken Wing Drumsticks, page 53
Cheese Caponata, page 63
Zucchini Bites, page 70
Open-Face Tacos, page 84
Homemade Soft Pretzels, page 128
Refried Bean Dip, page 121
Pita Bread, page 126

Mexican Party
Chili con Queso, page 27
Cheese-Chili Puffs, page 33
Jalapeño Pepper Jelly, page 68
California Onion Cakes, page 76
Mexican Pizza, page 33
Calico Mold, page 102
Guacamole Mold, page 99
Homemade Tortilla Chips, page 125
Guacamole, page 118
Party-Style Tostadas, page 119
North-of-the-Border Dip, page 122

Budget Entertaining
Poor Man's Pâté, page 94
Pickled Chili Spread, page 105
Curry Spread, page 109
Noodle Chips, page 125
Fresh Herb Dip, page 112
Herbed Eggs, page 39
Ranch-Style Bean Dip, page 28
Swiss Mustard Sausage, page 22

Meat Morsels

Bring exciting flavors from around the world to your appetizer tray by using the collection of meat morsels in this section. We've included flavor combinations tasted on our travels, in addition to those developed in our own test kitchen.

Purchase a few authentic Oriental ingredients for sparerib appetizers. They're sure to be voted favorites. Soy sauce is available in your neighborhood market. Hoisin sauce, which gives a distinct flavor to Far East Spareribs, can be found only in gourmet or Oriental sections of large supermarkets, in gourmet stores or Oriental markets. Chinese Barbecued Riblets are flavored with Chinese Five Spice Powder, a special blend of cinnamon, ginger, cloves, nutmeg and anise. You'll find it gives any meat an unusual degree of spiciness combined with a hint of licorice from the anise. In Plum-Glazed Spareribs, experience enchanting Oriental flavors using common plum jelly in the sauce.

Beef Yakitori was inspired by a group of popular appetizers from Japan. Thinly sliced meat is threaded on small bamboo sticks or skewers and marinated several hours to absorb flavors from the sauce before the meat is barbecued or broiled. Meat is easier to cut into thin slices if it is placed in the freezer until ice crystals form, making the meat firm. Use an electric slicing knife or electric rotary slicer to cut uniformly thin slices.

If you're heating up your backyard barbecue for the main part of dinner, use it to cook the broiled meat appetizers in this section. It will save energy and guests will have fun cooking their own succulent tidbits over the coals. Appetizer meats are small and dry out very rapidly over high heat. Keep the barbecue fire as low as possible and place the grill 5 to 8 inches from the flames or coals. Small bamboo sticks or skewers 4 to 6 inches long are ideal for mini-kabobs. They won't char or burn if you soak them in water before threading meat on the skewers.

Classic Sweet & Sour Meatballs

Serve these savory meatballs in a piquant sauce for your cocktail buffet main dish.

1 egg, slightly beaten
1/3 cup milk
1/2 cup soft breadcrumbs
1 teaspoon salt
1/8 teaspoon pepper

1/4 teaspoon ground sage
1/4 cup minced onion
1 lb. lean ground beef
Sweet & Sour Sauce, see below

Sweet & Sour Sauce:
1 (8-oz.) can sliced pineapple
2 tablespoons cornstarch
2 tablespoons soy sauce
1 cup chicken broth or bouillon

1/4 cup vinegar
1/4 cup honey
1 green pepper, cut in 1-inch squares

Preheat oven to 350°F (175°C). In a medium bowl, combine egg, milk, breadcrumbs, salt, pepper, sage and onion. Stir in ground beef. Shape into 1-inch balls. Arrange on a rack in broiler pan. Bake 15 to 20 minutes in preheated oven until lightly browned. Drain and discard drippings. Prepare Sweet & Sour Sauce. To serve, arrange meatballs in a chafing dish or heat-proof bowl on a hot tray. Pour sauce evenly over meatballs. Serve warm. Makes about 55 appetizer servings.

Sweet & Sour Sauce:
Drain pineapple; reserve juice in a small saucepan; set aside. Cut pineapple into 3/4-inch pieces; set aside. Stir cornstarch into reserved pineapple juice until dissolved. Stir in soy sauce, broth or bouillon, vinegar and honey. Cook and stir over medium-low heat until thickened and translucent. Stir in pineapple chunks and green pepper squares. Cook 1 minute longer.

Crunchy Meatballs

You'll enjoy these plain, but they are even better served with teriyaki sauce.

1 lb. lean ground beef
1/2 lb. lean ground pork
2 eggs, slightly beaten
1/2 teaspoon salt
1/4 cup fine dry breadcrumbs

1 tablespoon soy sauce
1/4 teaspoon garlic salt
1 (8-1/2-oz.) can water chestnuts,
    drained, finely chopped
1 cup teriyaki sauce, if desired

Preheat oven to 375°F (190°C). In a medium bowl, combine beef, pork, eggs, salt, breadcrumbs, soy sauce, garlic salt and water chestnuts. Shape into 1-inch balls. Arrange on a rack in broiler pan. Bake 15 to 18 minutes in preheated oven or until meatballs are browned throughout. Drain and discard drippings. Pour teriyaki sauce into a small bowl. To serve, spear warm baked meatballs with small wooden picks; dip into teriyaki sauce, if desired. Makes about 75 appetizers.

Rhineland Mini Fajitas

A marriage of unusual flavors that spell "wunderbar"

**2 thick pork loin chops
(about 1 to 1-1/2 lbs.)
1 teaspoon chili powder
1 garlic clove, crushed
1/2 teaspoon salt
1 tablespoon grated fresh gingerroot
1 tablespoon brown sugar
1/2 teaspoon grated orange peel
1 teaspoon Dijon-style mustard
1 tablespoon white wine vinegar**

**3 or 4 (9-inch) flour tortillas, quartered
1 tablespoon vegetable oil
1 tablespoon butter
1 medium onion, thinly sliced
1 medium red cooking apple, thinly sliced
1/3 cup dairy sour cream
Ground cinnamon
Orange peel
Parsley sprigs**

Remove bones from chops; trim fat. Place chops, 2 inches apart, between 2 sheets of plastic wrap or waxed paper. With a meat mallet, lightly pound pork to almost 1/2-inch thickness. Cut into 1/4-inch wide strips. Place strips in a single row, on a plate. In a small bowl, combine chili powder, garlic, salt, ginger, brown sugar and orange peel. Stir in mustard and wine vinegar. Lightly brush meat strips with spicy mixture. Cover and refrigerate at least 2 hours. Just before serving, wrap tortilla quarters in foil; heat in a 350F (175C) oven 15 minutes. Heat oil in a heavy 9-inch skillet. Add pork strips to skillet. Saute over medium-high heat until no longer pink when cut in thickest part; keep warm. Meanwhile, in another 8- or 9-inch skillet, melt butter over medium-high heat. Add onion and apple; cook stirring occasionally until onion is tender. To serve, spoon 2 or 3 strips of meat, down the center of each tortilla quarter; top with some apple-onion mixture. Roll up and secure with a wooden pick. Top with sour cream; then sprinkle with cinnamon and orange peel. Garnish with parsley sprigs. Makes 12 to 15 appetizer servings.

Sunset Ham Balls

Make up ham balls ahead of time and add them to the sauce just before serving.

**1 lb. lean cooked ham
1 egg
1 cup soft breadcrumbs
2 tablespoons chopped green onions
1 teaspoon minced parsley**

**1/8 teaspoon seasoned salt
1/2 teaspoon prepared mustard
1/2 cup barbecue sauce
1 (10-oz.) jar apricot-pineapple jam**

In food grinder or food processor, grind ham; set aside. Preheat oven to 350°F (175°C). In a medium bowl, beat egg slightly. Stir in breadcrumbs, onions, parsley, seasoned salt and mustard. Stir in ground ham. Shape into 1-inch balls. Arrange ham balls on a rack in a broiler pan. Bake about 15 minutes in preheated oven until lightly browned. In a large skillet or stovetop casserole, combine barbecue sauce and jam; stir over medium heat until blended. Add cooked ham balls; heat until bubbly. Serve hot in stovetop casserole or spoon into a chafing dish. Makes 35 to 40 appetizer servings.

Luau Meatballs   Photo on pages 30 and 31.

Perfect for Hawaiian parties.

1 lb. lean ground pork
1 (6-oz.) can water chestnuts, drained,
    finely chopped
1/4 cup finely chopped green onions
1/2 teaspoon salt

1/2 teaspoon Worcestershire sauce
1/3 cup fine dry breadcrumbs
1 egg, beaten
Luau Sauce, see below

Luau Sauce:
1 cup unsweetened pineapple juice
1/4 cup dry white wine
1/2 cup chicken broth or bouillon
2 tablespoons packed brown sugar

2 teaspoons finely chopped crystallized
    ginger
1 tablespoon cornstarch
1 tablespoon soy sauce

Preheat oven to 375°F (190°C). In a medium bowl, combine pork, water chestnuts, onions, salt, Worcestershire sauce and breadcrumbs. Use a fork to stir in egg until thoroughly combined. Shape mixture into 1-inch balls. Arrange on a rack in a broiler pan. Bake 30 to 35 minutes in preheated oven until lightly browned throughout. Drain and discard drippings. Prepare Luau Sauce. Arrange cooked meatballs in a chafing dish or heat-proof dish on a hot tray. Pour sauce over meatballs; serve hot. Makes 60 to 65 appetizer servings.

Luau Sauce:
In a small saucepan, combine pineapple juice, wine, chicken broth or bouillon, brown sugar and ginger. Bring to boil. Dissolve cornstarch in soy sauce; stir into hot pineapple mixture. Cook and stir over medium heat until slightly thickened.

Far East Spareribs

Dark red and spicy hoisin sauce is made from soybeans, garlic, spices and other seasonings.

3 to 4 lbs. pork spareribs
1/3 cup honey
1/4 cup soy sauce

1 garlic clove, crushed
1/4 cup hoisin sauce
1/2 teaspoon dry mustard

Have your butcher cut ribs crosswise. Cut between bones to separate ribs. In a large saucepan, cover cut ribs with lightly salted water. Cover and simmer 30 minutes. Drain; set aside. In a small bowl, combine honey, soy sauce, garlic, hoisin sauce and mustard; set aside. Preheat broiler if necessary. Place oven rack 5 to 8 inches from heating element. Place a rack in a broiler pan or on a large baking sheet with raised sides. Arrange cooked ribs in single layer on rack. Brush ribs with sauce; broil until golden brown, about 2 minutes. Turn meat, brush with sauce and broil on other side about 2 minutes until golden brown. Arrange broiled ribs on a large platter; serve warm. Makes 35 to 40 appetizer servings.

Chinese Barbecued Riblets

Chinese five spice powder and hoisin sauce are available in Oriental food markets.

3 lbs. pork spareribs
1/2 cup soy sauce
1 garlic clove, crushed
1/2 cup hoisin sauce
1/2 cup dry white wine

1/2 teaspoon ground ginger
1/2 teaspoon Chinese 5 spice powder
3 or 4 drops red food coloring,
  if desired

Have your butcher cut ribs crosswise. Cut between bones to separate ribs. In a large saucepan, cover separated riblets with lightly salted water. Cover and simmer 30 minutes over medium-low heat. Drain; place cooked ribs in a large non-metal bowl. Set aside. In a small bowl, combine soy sauce, garlic, hoisin sauce, wine, ginger, 5 spice powder and red food coloring, if desired. Pour over drained meat. Cover and marinate 3 to 4 hours in refrigerator, turning occasionally. Drain; reserve marinade. Preheat broiler or barbecue grill, if necessary. Place a rack in a broiler pan or on barbecue grill. Arrange drained meat on rack. Turning once, broil until browned and crisp. While broiling, brush each side with marinade at least once. Arrange on a platter; serve hot. Makes 30 to 35 appetizer servings.

Plum-Glazed Spareribs   Photo on pages 30 and 31.

This is a short-cut method to make plum sauce.

3 to 3-1/2 lbs. pork spareribs
1/4 cup soy sauce
2 tablespoons honey
2 tablespoons lemon juice

1 garlic clove, crushed
1/4 cup dry white wine
Plum Sauce, see below
1/4 cup toasted sesame seeds

Plum Sauce:
1 cup plum jelly
2 tablespoons vinegar

2 tablespoons ketchup

Have your butcher cut ribs crosswise. Cut between bones to separate ribs. Place separated ribs in a large non-metal bowl; set aside. In a small bowl, combine soy sauce, honey, lemon juice, garlic and wine. Pour over ribs. Cover and marinate 6 hours or overnight in refrigerator. Preheat oven to 375°F (190°C). Drain ribs; discard marinade. Arrange marinated ribs in a 15" x 10" baking sheet with raised sides. Cover and bake 45 minutes. Prepare Plum Sauce. Brush sauce over baked ribs. Bake 10 minutes uncovered. Turn ribs; brush with sauce. Sprinkle with sesame seeds. Bake uncovered 10 minutes longer. Arrange baked ribs on a large platter; serve hot. Makes 30 to 35 appetizer servings.

Plum Sauce:
In a small saucepan, combine jelly, vinegar and ketchup. Stir over low heat until jelly melts.

Korean-Style Beef & Mushrooms

For economy, use smaller pieces of meat and several fresh pineapple chunks on each skewer.

1 lb. boneless top sirloin steak
15 to 20 small mushrooms
2 tablespoons vegetable oil
1/4 cup soy sauce
1 garlic clove, crushed
1/4 cup minced onion

1/8 teaspoon pepper
1 (1/4-inch) slice fresh ginger root,
   finely chopped, or
   1/4 teaspoon ground ginger
1 teaspoon honey

Have your butcher cut steak into 15 to 20 very thin slices or partially freeze steak and cut into very thin slices. Thread meat on fifteen to twenty 6-inch bamboo skewers by pushing skewers in and out of each meat slice as though sewing. Thread a mushroom on 1 end of each skewer; set aside. In a 9'' x 5'' loaf pan, combine oil, soy sauce, garlic, onion, pepper, ginger and honey. Place skewered meat in marinade, turning to coat all sides. Cover and refrigerate 6 hours or overnight. Turn occasionally. Drain, reserving marinade. Preheat broiler or barbecue grill, if necessary. Place oven rack 5 to 8 inches from heating element. Broil meat in oven or on grill about 2 minutes. Baste several times with reserved marinade. Turn and baste with marinade; broil until evenly browned. Serve hot. Makes 15 to 20 appetizer servings.

Beef Yakitori

These tasty morsels are similar to Japan's favorite appetizer.

1/2 cup soy sauce
2 tablespoons lemon juice
2 tablespoons sugar
1 garlic clove, crushed
1/2 teapoon ground ginger

2 tablespoons vegetable oil
1 teaspoon sesame seeds
2 green onions, finely chopped
1 lb. beef sirloin, thinly sliced

In a 9'' x 5'' loaf pan, combine soy sauce, lemon juice, sugar, garlic, ginger, oil, sesame seeds and onions. Thread meat on eighteen to twenty 6-inch bamboo skewers by pushing a skewer in and out of each meat slice as though sewing. Place skewered meat in marinade, turning to coat all sides. Cover and refrigerate 3 to 4 hours; drain. Arrange marinated skewered meat on broiler pan or ungreased baking sheet with raised sides. Preheat broiler if necessary. Place oven rack 5 to 8 inches from heating element. Broil meat 1-1/2 to 2 minutes; turn and broil about 1 minute longer. Serve hot. Makes 18 to 20 appetizer servings.

How to Make Korean-Style Beef & Mushrooms

1/Use a very sharp knife to cut partially frozen meat into very thin slices.

2/Thread 1 meat slice and 1 mushroom on each skewer. Marinate at least 6 hours.

Teriyaki Roll-Ups

Partially frozen beef holds its shape and is easier to cut into thin slices.

1/3 cup soy sauce
2 tablespoons honey
1/4 teaspoon ground ginger
1 garlic clove, crushed
1 teaspoon grated onion

1/4 cup dry white wine
3/4 lb. boneless top sirloin or
  fillet of beef
1 (6-oz.) can water chestnuts, drained

In a shallow medium bowl, combine soy sauce, honey, ginger, garlic, onion and wine; set aside. Cut meat into very thin diagonal slices. Cut water chestnuts in half. Wrap 1 slice meat around each water chestnut half. Secure with a wooden pick. Marinate in soy sauce mixture 1 hour. Preheat broiler if necessary. Place oven rack 5 to 8 inches from heating element. Remove marinated roll-ups from marinade; arrange on broiler pan. Discard marinade. Turning once or twice, broil meat 3 to 4 minutes until evenly browned. Serve hot. Makes 40 to 45 appetizer servings.

When barbecuing mini-kabobs, prevent charring or burning of wooden skewers by soaking them in water before threading meat on them.

Indonesian Pork Sate

You'll need six-inch bamboo skewers for these spicy mini-kabobs.

1-1/2 lbs. lean boneless pork
1 cup peanuts, roasted, salted
1/2 cup chopped green onions
2 tablespoons lemon juice
2 tablespoons honey
1/4 cup soy sauce

1 garlic clove, chopped
1 teaspoon coriander seeds
1/2 teaspoon crumbled dried red peppers
1/2 cup chicken broth or bouillon
1/4 cup butter, melted

Trim and discard fat from pork. Cut pork into 1-inch cubes. Thread 3 or 4 pork cubes on each of twenty to twenty-five 6-inch bamboo skewers. Layer skewered meat in an 8-inch square baking dish; set aside. In blender, combine peanuts, onions, lemon juice, honey, soy sauce, garlic, coriander seeds and red peppers. Process until almost smooth. Add broth or bouillon and butter. Process 3 to 4 seconds to blend. Pour over skewered pork cubes. Marinate 6 hours or overnight in refrigerator. Drain; reserve marinade. Preheat broiler or barbecue grill, if necessary. Place oven rack 5 to 8 inches from heating element. Place a wire rack in a broiler pan or on barbecue grill. Arrange marinated meat on rack. Broil until browned and crisp, about 5 minutes. Turn and brush with marinade; broil until browned on all sides, 4 to 5 minutes. Arrange on a large platter; serve hot. Makes 20 to 25 appetizer servings.

Mushroom-Burger Bites

Their unique shape and exceptional flavor will stimulate conversation.

1/2 lb. medium mushrooms (30 to 35)
1/4 lb. lean ground beef
1/8 teaspoon salt
Pinch pepper
1/8 teaspoon dried oregano leaves,
   crushed

2 tablespoons ketchup
30 to 35 Melba toast rounds
1 (6-oz.) pkg. sliced mozzarella cheese
   (about 3 slices)

Wipe mushrooms with a damp cloth. Remove and finely chop mushroom stems. In a small skillet, cook and stir ground beef until browned. Add chopped mushroom stems, salt, pepper and oregano. Sauté 2 to 3 minutes until mushroom stems are tender. Drain and discard drippings. Stir in ketchup. Spoon about 1 tablespoon meat mixture on top of each toast round. Arrange toast rounds on an ungreased baking sheet. Place 1 mushroom cap, rounded-side up, on top of each toast round. Cut cheese into wedges large enough to cover mushroom but no larger than toast. Place 1 cheese wedge on top of each mushroom cap. Refrigerate. To serve, preheat oven to 350°F (175°C). Bake appetizers 10 to 15 minutes until cheese melts and meat mixture is hot. Arrange on a large platter; serve hot. Makes 30 to 35 appetizer servings.

Ham & Pineapple Kabobs

Use a pastry brush or a small paint brush to apply the jelly sauce.

40 (3/4-inch) cubes cooked ham
  (about 2 cups)
1 (16-oz.) can pineapple chunks, drained
1/2 cup chili sauce

1 tablespoon cornstarch
1/2 cup currant jelly
1 teaspoon prepared mustard
1/2 teaspoon grated orange peel

Arrange ham and pineapple alternately on twenty 6-inch bamboo skewers; set aside. In a small saucepan, combine chili sauce and cornstarch. Stir in jelly, mustard and orange peel. Cook and stir over low heat until thickened. Preheat broiler or barbecue grill, if necessary. Place oven rack 5 to 8 inches from heating element. Place a wire rack in a broiler pan. Arrange skewered ham and pineapple on rack; brush with jelly sauce. Turning and brushing with sauce several times, broil about 3 minutes until hot. Arrange broiled kabobs on a large platter; serve warm. Makes 20 appetizer servings.

How to Make Mushroom & Burger Bites

1/Spread about 1 tablespoon meat mixture evenly over each Melba toast round.

2/Arrange on baking sheet. Top each with 1 mushroom cap and 1 cheese triangle.

Golden West Tidbits

These flavors are reminiscent of the Orient.

3/4 lb. sliced bacon (about 11 slices)
1 (8-oz.) jar preserved kumquats
1 (6-oz.) can water chestnuts, drained
1/4 cup soy sauce

2 tablespoons white wine vinegar
1 tablespoon honey
1/4 teaspoon garlic salt

Cut each bacon slice in half crosswise. Drain kumquats, reserving 2 tablespoons syrup. Cut each kumquat in half lengthwise; scoop out and discard seeds. Place 1 water chestnut in each kumquat half. Wrap 1 bacon slice around each filled kumquat; secure with a small wooden pick. Place in a medium bowl. In a small bowl or measuring cup, combine soy sauce, vinegar, honey, garlic salt and reserved kumquat syrup. Pour over bacon-wrapped kumquats. Cover and refrigerate 4 to 6 hours; drain. Preheat oven to 375°F (190°C). Place a rack in a broiler pan or in an ungreased baking sheet with raised sides. Arrange drained marinated tidbits on rack. Bake 25 to 35 minutes in preheated oven or until bacon is crisp. Makes 20 to 22 appetizer servings.

Swiss Mustard Sausage

Serve this hearty mustard-flavored snack with cold beer.

1 lb. unsliced salami or summer sausage
1/2 cup dry red wine
2 green onions, finely chopped
1/8 teaspoon pepper

1/4 teaspoon salt
Pinch ground allspice
1/4 cup prepared mustard

Remove rind from salami or summer sausage; cut into eighty to ninety 3/4-inch cubes; set aside. In a small saucepan, combine wine, onions, pepper, salt, allspice and mustard. Bring to boil; simmer over low heat 2 to 3 minutes until onions are soft. Add salami or summer sausage pieces; heat until mixture begins to bubble. Pour into a chafing dish or heat-proof bowl on a hot tray; keep warm. Makes 80 to 90 appetizer servings.

Ham Rolls

You'll enjoy the spicy filling with a sweet and sour flavor.

1 teaspoon dry mustard
2 tablespoons pineapple-apricot jam

1 teaspoon chopped chives
12 slices boiled or baked ham

In a small bowl, combine mustard, jam and chives. Spread evenly on ham slices. Roll up jelly-roll fashion. Cut each crosswise into 3 equal pieces. Secure with small wooden picks. Makes 36 appetizer servings.

Chutney Rumaki

There is no liver in this spicy fruit version of traditional rumaki.

1 lb. sliced bacon
1 tablespoon prepared mustard
2 tablespoons brown sugar

1/4 cup chutney
1 (8-oz.) can water chestnuts, drained

Cook bacon until most of the fat is removed but bacon is still soft. Drain on paper towels. Lightly spread one side of each bacon slice with mustard. Sprinkle evenly with brown sugar; set aside. Remove fruit from chutney and chop very fine. Return chopped fruit to chutney syrup. Dip each water chestnut into chutney. With coated side up, wrap a bacon slice around each water chestnut; secure ends of bacon with small wooden picks. Preheat oven to 400°F (205°C). Arrange bacon-wrapped water chestnuts in a 13" x 9" baking pan. Bake 5 to 10 minutes in preheated oven until bacon is crisp. Serve warm. Makes 14 to 16 appetizer servings.

Spicy Dog Bites

Teenagers enjoy preparing this in a stove-to-table casserole, chafing dish or fondue pot.

1 (16-oz.) pkg. frankfurters
1/2 cup currant jelly
1/2 cup chili sauce

1 teaspoon prepared mustard
1 teaspoon dried minced onion

Cut each frankfurter crosswise into 5 or 6 equal pieces. Place in a chafing dish or stove-top cassserole over low heat. In a small saucepan, combine currant jelly, chili sauce, mustard and onion. Stir over low heat until jelly melts. Pour over frankfurter pieces; serve warm. Makes 50 to 60 appetizer servings.

Use lean ground beef in appetizers or pour off excess drippings after meat is cooked.

Cheese & Egg Tempters

Clever party-givers serve at least one cheese appetizer because everyone likes cheese. Cream cheese is a favorite and is used in almost any mixture. It is especially good in flavorful dips, creamy spreads and tangy cheese logs. Firm cheeses such as Monterey Jack, sharp Cheddar and Swiss add excellent flavor to logs and spreads.

Emmentaler is the original fondue cheese, but Cheddar is popular because it also melts evenly and blends with other ingredients. Serve fondue when you want to radiate a warm and friendly atmosphere. It can be kept warm in a fondue pot or chafing dish or on a hot tray. Grated cheese blends into sauces better than chunks or julienned pieces. **Never boil cheese mixtures.** Cheese becomes stringy and tough at high temperatures. When you serve fondue, set the pattern for others by swirling your bread cube on a long fork in a figure-8 pattern through the fondue. This helps keep the fondue blended and smooth and at the same time coats the bread with the warm melted-cheese mixture.

Most cheeses keep well in the refrigerator two weeks to three months if they are wrapped airtight. Cheese you plan to use in fondues or sauces can be frozen up to six months, then thawed slowly in the refrigerator. After it has been frozen, cheese sometimes crumbles.

Use hard-cooked eggs as a base for spreads or as an extender. For seven marvelous deviled-egg ideas, see the variations to Basic Deviled Eggs. Try the subtle flavors of curry and chutney, bacon and cheese or smoky cheese spread and mustard. For a really different look, add the juice of pickled beets to the mashed egg yolks to make Rosy Eggs. Give deviled eggs a festive and professional look by piping the rosy colored egg-yolk mixture through a pastry bag into the egg whites. Decorate deviled eggs with anchovies, herbs or caviar. Use these elaborately decorated eggs to add interest to an appetizer tray.

Stuffed Edam

The shiny, red-coated cheese shell makes an attractive serving piece.

1 (1-lb.) whole Edam cheese,
   room temperature
1/4 cup mayonnaise
2 teaspoons chopped chives

2 tablespoons dry white wine
2 teaspoons chopped parsley
2 oz. Swiss cheese, cut in pieces

Cut a 2-1/2-inch circle from top of Edam cheese. Remove and discard circle of red coating. Scoop out center of cheese, leaving about 1/4-inch shell; leave coating intact. Place pieces of removed cheese in food processor or blender. Add mayonnaise, chives, wine, parsley and Swiss cheese. Process until smooth. Spoon about 2/3 of cheese mixture evenly into cheese shell. Refrigerate remaining cheese mixture; use to refill shell. Makes about 1-3/4 cups.

Blue Cheese Balls

Blue cheese is similar to French Roquefort and is made almost worldwide.

4 oz. blue cheese, crumbled
1/2 cup butter
1 cup all-purpose flour

1/2 teaspoon seasoned salt
Dash hot pepper sauce
1/2 cup finely chopped blanched almonds

Preheat oven to 375°F (190°C). In a small bowl, cream blue cheese and butter. Beat in flour, seasoned salt and hot pepper sauce. Shape into 1-inch balls. Roll in almonds; flatten slightly. Arrange on an ungreased baking sheet. Bake about 12 minutes in preheated oven until lightly browned. Serve warm. Makes about 35 appetizer servings.

Use two forks to crumble soft cheeses. Pull them apart as though shredding cooked meat.

Peppered Cheese

Seasoned pepper contains black and sweet peppers with a variety of herbs and spices.

**2 cups grated Monterey Jack cheese
    (8 oz.)**
**1 (8-oz.) pkg. cream cheese,
    room temperature**
1 teaspoon fines herbes

1 teaspoon minced chives
1 teaspoon Worcestershire sauce
1 garlic clove, crushed
2 to 3 tablespoons seasoned pepper
Plain or bacon-flavored crackers

In a medium bowl, combine Monterey Jack cheese, cream cheese, fines herbes, chives, Worcestershire sauce and garlic. Shape cheese mixture into a 5-inch ball; slightly flatten 1 side. Cut a 12-inch square of waxed paper. On a flat surface, spread seasoned pepper in an even thick layer on waxed paper. Roll cheese ball in pepper until completely covered. Refrigerate 6 hours or overnight. Cheese ball can be stored in refrigerator several days before serving. Cut into thin slices; serve on crackers. Makes one 5-inch cheese ball.

Smoky Cheese Log

Serve this savory mixture with crackers or fresh fruit or use it to stuff celery.

**2 cups grated sharp Cheddar cheese
    (8 oz.)**
2 cups grated Swiss cheese (8 oz.)
1/2 cup mayonnaise
1 teaspoon grated onion

1 garlic clove, crushed
1 teaspoon Worcestershire sauce
1/4 teaspoon celery salt
1/8 teaspoon liquid smoke seasoning
2 to 3 drops hot pepper sauce

In a medium bowl, combine Cheddar cheese and Swiss cheese. Stir in mayonnaise until evenly distributed. Stir in remaining ingredients. Shape into a 9" x 3" log; wrap airtight in plastic wrap or foil. Refrigerate 3 to 4 hours to blend flavors. Makes 1 cheese log.

Chili con Queso

Serve corn chips, crackers or cubes of French bread with this delightful Mexican dip.

1 lb. sharp Cheddar cheese
**2 fresh or canned California green
    chilies, seeded**
2 green onions

1 garlic clove
1 (8-oz.) can tomatoes
1/2 teaspoon salt
1/2 teaspoon Worcestershire sauce

Cut cheese, chilies and onions into chunks. In blender or food processor, combine all ingredients. Process 5 to 10 seconds or until finely chopped. Pour into a medium saucepan or chafing dish; heat until cheese melts. Serve hot in chafing dish, fondue pot or bowl on a hot tray. Makes about 3 cups.

Peppered Cheese

Ranch-Style Bean Dip

Spicy but not too hot.

1/4 cup butter or margarine
1 small onion, chopped
1 jalapeño pepper, seeded,
 finely chopped
1 garlic clove, crushed

1 (16-oz.) can pinto beans or
 kidney beans, drained
1 cup grated Monterey Jack cheese (4 oz.)
Corn chips for dipping

In a medium skillet, melt butter or margarine. Add onion, jalapeño pepper and garlic; sauté until tender. In a medium bowl, use a fork to mash beans. Stir into onion mixture. Cook and stir over low heat until hot but not boiling. Stir in cheese until melted; do not boil. Spoon into a small fondue pot or small bowl on a hot tray. Serve hot with corn chips for dipping. Makes about 2 cups.

Cheese Fondue

You can substitute other cheeses for the Gruyère, but don't use a process cheese.

1 garlic clove
1 cup dry white wine
2 cups grated Swiss cheese (8 oz.)
1 cup grated Gruyère cheese (4 oz.)
1/4 teaspoon dry mustard

2 teaspoons cornstarch
1 tablespoon Cognac or kirsch
1 small loaf French bread,
 cut in 1-inch cubes

Cut garlic clove in half. Rub cut surface of garlic over side and bottom of a fondue pot or a heavy medium saucepan; discard garlic. Pour wine into fondue pot or saucepan. Place over low heat until bubbles rise to surface. In a medium bowl, combine Swiss cheese, Gruyère cheese, mustard and cornstarch. Slowly stir cheese mixture into hot wine until mixture is blended and smooth. Gradually stir in Cognac or kirsch. Keep warm over very low heat. To serve, use fondue forks to swirl French bread through warm mixture in a figure-8 pattern. Makes about 2-1/2 cups.

Spicy Cheese Fondue

Cheese fondue with a bite to it.

1/4 cup butter or margarine
1/4 cup all-purpose flour
1 cup milk
1 cup beer
2 teaspoons dry mustard
4 teaspoons steak sauce

1/4 teaspoon paprika
1/4 teaspoon salt
6 to 8 dashes hot pepper sauce
4 cups grated Cheddar cheese (1 lb.)
1 loaf French bread, cut in 1-inch cubes

In a medium saucepan, melt butter or margarine. Stir in flour until bubbly. Slowly stir in milk and beer. Cook and stir over low heat 4 to 5 minutes until slightly thickened. In a small bowl, combine mustard, steak sauce, paprika, salt and hot pepper sauce. Stir into white sauce. Over low heat, gradually stir in cheese; do not boil. Keep hot in chafing dish or on hot tray. To serve, use fondue forks to swirl French bread through hot mixture in a figure-8 pattern. Makes 4 cups.

Cheese Fritters

Serve these warm to fully enjoy the delicate cheese flavor.

1/4 cup butter or margarine
1/2 cup water
1/2 cup all-purpose flour
1/2 teaspoon baking powder
1/8 teaspoon salt
2 eggs

1/2 cup grated Cheddar cheese (2 oz.)
1/4 cup grated Parmesan cheese (1 oz.)
2 egg whites
Oil for deep-frying
Additional grated Parmesan cheese,
    if desired

In a medium saucepan, heat butter or margarine and water to a rolling boil. In a small bowl, combine flour, baking powder and salt. Add to water mixture all at once. Beat vigorously over low heat about 1 minute until mixture becomes smooth and leaves side of pan. Remove from heat. Beat in eggs, one at a time. Continue to beat until mixture has lost its sheen. Beat in Cheddar cheese and 1/4 cup Parmesan cheese. In a medium bowl, beat egg whites until stiff but not dry. Fold into cheese mixture. Pour oil into a deep-fryer to depth recommended by manufacturer or pour oil 2 inches deep in a heavy medium saucepan. Heat oil to 375°F (190°C). At this temperature a 1-inch cube of bread will turn golden brown in 40 seconds. Carefully drop heaping teaspoonfuls of cheese mixture into hot oil. Fry until puffy and golden, 40 to 50 seconds. Use a slotted spoon to remove cooked fritters from hot oil; drain on paper towels. Sprinkle with additional grated Parmesan cheese, if desired. Serve warm. Makes about 35 appetizer servings.

Beachcomber Quiche

This contains quiche ingredients, but there's no crust to make!

3 eggs
1 (3-oz.) pkg. cream cheese,
    room temperature
1 cup cottage cheese
1/4 cup butter
1/4 cup all-purpose flour

1/2 teaspoon baking powder
1/4 teaspoon salt
1/2 cup milk
1 cup grated Cheddar cheese (4 oz.)
1/2 cup chopped cooked bacon or ham

Grease a 9-inch pie pan; set aside. Preheat oven to 350°F (175°C). In a large bowl, beat eggs. Beat in cream cheese, cottage cheese and butter until almost smooth. In a small bowl, combine flour, baking powder and salt. Stir into egg mixture until thoroughly blended. Beat in milk until thoroughly blended. Pour evenly into prepared pie pan. Sprinkle evenly with Cheddar cheese and bacon or ham. Bake 30 to 40 minutes in preheated oven until mixture is firm in center. Cut into 12 to 15 small wedges; serve warm. Makes 12 to 15 appetizer servings.

On following pages: South Sea Buffet. Clockwise from right, Plum-Glazed Spareribs, page 17; Aloha Loaf, page 100; on board, Buffet Salmon & Cucumber Sauce, page 45; in red casserole, Luau Meatballs, page 16.

Mediterranean Sampler

Feta is a white, salty cheese originally from Greece but now available in many countries.

5 eggs
1/2 cup plain yogurt
1/2 teaspoon salt
2 green onions, finely chopped
1 tablespoon minced parsley

1/4 cup crumbled feta cheese
4 slices pepperoni sausage,
 finely chopped
1 tablespoon sesame seeds

Grease an 8-inch square baking pan; set aside. Preheat oven to 350°F (175°C). In a medium bowl, beat eggs until pale and thickened. Stir in yogurt, salt, onions, parsley, cheese and pepperoni. Pour evenly into prepared pan. Sprinkle with sesame seeds. Bake 15 to 20 minutes in preheated oven until just set. Cut into 8 horizontal rows and 7 or 8 vertical rows. Makes 56 to 64 appetizer servings.

Smoky Rounds

Use the plastic blade in your food processor for fast preparation.

1 (8-oz.) pkg. cold-pack smoky
 cheese spread
1/2 cup butter or margarine
1 cup all-purpose flour

1/2 teaspoon prepared mustard
1 cup finely chopped cooked ham
1/2 teaspoon Worcestershire sauce

In a medium bowl, combine cheese spread and butter or margarine. Stir in flour until thoroughly blended. Stir in mustard, ham and Worcestershire sauce. Preheat oven to 350°F (175°C). Shape cheese spread mixture into 1-inch balls. Arrange on an ungreased baking sheet. Bake 12 to 15 minutes in preheated oven until golden brown. Makes about 60 appetizer servings.

Baja Bites

Similar to quiche but the flavor of Baja, California.

5 eggs
1 cup cottage cheese
1/4 cup all-purpose flour
1/2 teaspoon baking powder
1/4 cup butter, melted

2 tablespoons minced green onions
1 (4-oz.) can chopped green chilies,
 drained
2 cups grated Monterey Jack cheese
 (8 oz.)

Grease an 8-inch square baking pan; set aside. Preheat oven to 350°F (175°C). In a large bowl, beat eggs. Add cottage cheese; beat until almost smooth. Beat in flour, baking powder and melted butter until thoroughly blended. Stir in onions, chilies and Monterey Jack cheese. Pour evenly into prepared pan. Bake 30 to 40 minutes in preheated oven until firm in center. Let cool slightly. Cut into 5 rows horizontally and 5 rows vertically; serve warm. Makes 25 appetizer servings.

Mexican Pizza

This chili relleno flavored pizza bakes firm without a crust.

1/4 cup all-purpose flour	1 (4-oz.) can chopped green chilies
1/2 teaspoon salt	1 cup cottage cheese
1/4 cup butter or margarine, melted	2 cups grated Monterey Jack cheese
4 eggs, slightly beaten	(8 oz.)

Grease a 12-inch pizza pan; set aside. Preheat oven to 375°F (190°C). In a medium bowl, combine flour, salt and melted butter or margarine. Stir in eggs, chilies, cottage cheese and Monterey Jack cheese. Pour evenly into greased pan. Bake 15 to 20 minutes in preheated oven until firm and lightly browned. Cut into thin wedges. Makes 16 to 18 appetizer servings.

Cheese-Chili Puffs

You'll enjoy these spicy, puffed cookie-like cheese wafers.

1-3/4 cups all-purpose flour	1/2 cup dairy sour cream
1/2 teaspoon seasoned salt	1 cup grated sharp Cheddar cheese
1/2 teaspoon garlic salt	(4 oz.)
1/2 cup butter or margarine	1/4 cup chopped green chilies, drained

In a medium bowl, combine flour, seasoned salt and garlic salt. Use a pastry blender or fork to cut in butter or margarine until mixture is crumbly. Stir in sour cream until mixture holds together. Stir in cheese and chilies. Shape into a ball. Cover and refrigerate 6 hours or overnight. Preheat oven to 375°F (190°C). On a lightly floured board, roll out dough 1/4 inch thick. Cut into 1-1/2-inch circles or into fancy shapes with cookie cutters. Place on an ungreased baking sheet. Bake 14 to 18 minutes in preheated oven until puffed and golden. Serve immediately. Makes about 60 appetizer servings.

Swiss Olive Morsels

Black olives, red pimiento and yellow cheese make these appetizers colorful.

6 eggs	1 tablespoon chopped pimiento
1/3 cup all-purpose flour	1 cup cottage cheese
1/2 teaspoon baking powder	2 cups grated Swiss cheese (8 oz.)
1/2 teaspoon garlic salt	1/4 cup butter or margarine, melted
1/2 cup chopped ripe olives	

Grease an 8-inch square baking pan; set aside. Preheat oven to 375°F (190°C). In a large bowl, beat eggs. Stir in flour, baking powder and garlic salt. Add olives, pimiento, cottage cheese, Swiss cheese and melted butter or margarine; stir until just blended. Spoon evenly into prepared pan. Bake 40 to 50 minutes in preheated oven until firm in center; cool slightly. Cut 8 horizontal rows and 5 vertical rows. Serve warm. Makes about 40 appetizer servings.

Dilly Cheese Cubes

Refrigerate or freeze these soft-centered cubes and bake them later.

1 loaf French bread, unsliced
1/2 cup butter
4 cups grated Cheddar cheese (1 lb.)
2 teaspoons dried dill weed

1 teaspoon Worcestershire sauce
1 tablespoon grated onion
2 eggs, slightly beaten

Remove crust from bread; reserve crusts for another purpose. Cut bread into 1-inch cubes; set aside. In a medium saucepan, stir butter and cheese over low heat until melted. Stir in dill weed, Worcestershire sauce and onion. Use a whisk or electric mixer to beat in eggs. Using a fork, dip each bread cube into hot cheese mixture, turning to coat all sides. Shake off excess sauce. Arrange coated cubes on an ungreased baking sheet. Refrigerate 1 to 2 days or freeze immediately. Store frozen cubes in airtight containers up to 6 months. To serve, preheat oven to 350°F (175°C). Bake refrigerated cheese cubes 10 minutes, frozen cheese cubes 15 minutes. Serve hot. Makes about 65 appetizer servings.

Calico Cheese Fingers

These are easier to handle if you cut the open-face sandwiches after they're broiled.

1/4 cup grated Monterey Jack cheese
  (1 oz.)
1/4 cup grated Parmesan cheese (1 oz.)
1/2 cup mayonnaise

1/4 cup finely chopped red onion
2 tablespoons minced parsley
8 slices white or wheat sandwich bread

In a small bowl, combine Monterey Jack cheese, Parmesan cheese, mayonnaise, onion and parsley; set aside. Preheat broiler if necessary. Place oven shelf 3 to 6 inches from heating element. Cut crusts from bread; reserve crusts for another purpose. Toast 1 side of trimmed bread slices. Spread cheese mixture on untoasted side. Broil until cheese mixture bubbles. Cut each slice of bread horizontally into 3 thin strips. Serve warm. Makes 24 appetizer servings.

How to Make Dilly Cheese Cubes

1/Using a long kitchen fork or fondue fork, dip bread cubes into hot cheese sauce; shake off excess sauce.

2/Bake refrigerated cubes or freeze on baking sheet then wrap airtight and store in freezer.

Toasted Cheese Roll-Ups

Sandwich bread is easier to roll up than thicker slices of bread.

1 cup grated Monterey Jack cheese (4 oz.)
1/4 cup mayonnaise
1/4 cup chopped ripe olives
1 teaspoon dried minced onion

1/4 teaspoon seasoned salt
12 slices sandwich bread
1/4 cup butter or margarine, melted

In a small bowl, combine cheese, mayonnaise, olives, onion and seasoned salt. Preheat oven to 450°F (230°C). Cut crusts from bread slices; use crusts for another purpose. Use a rolling pin to flatten each bread slice to a 5-inch square. Spread about 1 tablespoon cheese mixture on each slice of flattened bread. Carefully roll up jelly-roll fashion. Cut each roll into 3 crosswise pieces. Arrange seam-side down on an ungreased baking sheet. Brush with melted butter or margarine. Bake 5 to 7 minutes in preheated oven until toasted. Serve hot. Makes 36 appetizer servings.

Olive & Cheese Squares

Make these squares more colorful with a garnish of sliced ripe olives and pimiento strips.

1 (4-1/4 oz.) can chopped ripe olives,
   drained
2 cups grated sharp Cheddar cheese
   (8 oz.)

2 tablespoons mayonnaise
2 green onions, finely chopped
1/2 teaspoon seasoned salt
12 slices white or wheat sandwich bread

In a medium bowl, combine olives, cheese, mayonnaise, onions and seasoned salt; set aside. Preheat broiler if necessary. Place oven shelf 3 to 6 inches from heating element. Cut crusts from bread; reserve crusts for another use. Lightly toast bread. Spread about 2 tablespoons olive mixture over each slice. Cut each slice into 4 squares. Arrange squares on an ungreased baking sheet. Broil until topping bubbles, 2 to 3 minutes. Serve hot. Makes 48 appetizer servings.

Appetizer Cheese Bars

These party-size bars are made in a jelly-roll pan for easy cutting.

1 envelope active dry yeast
1/4 cup warm water (110°F, 45°C)
2 eggs
1/4 cup butter or margarine,
   room temperature

1 tablespoon sugar
1/2 teaspoon salt
1/3 cup warm milk (110°F, 45°C)
2-1/2 cups all-purpose flour
Herb-Cheese Filling, see below

Herb-Cheese Filling:
2 cups ricotta cheese (16 oz.)
2/3 cup grated Parmesan cheese
   (about 3-1/2 oz.)
2 eggs, slightly beaten

2 tablespoons minced chives
2 tablespoons minced parsley
1/2 teaspoon dried marjoram leaves,
   crushed

In a small bowl or measuring cup, sprinkle yeast over warm water. Stir to soften yeast. Let stand about 5 minutes until dissolved. In a large bowl, beat eggs; stir in butter or margarine, sugar, salt, warm milk, dissolved yeast and 1 cup flour. Beat until smooth. Gradually stir in remaining flour. Shape into a ball. Turn out onto a lightly floured board; let rest while cleaning and greasing bowl. Knead 5 to 7 minutes or until smooth. Place in greased bowl, turning to grease top. Cover and set in warm place; let rise 1 to 1-1/2 hours or until doubled in volume. Grease a large baking sheet with raised sides; set aside. Punch down dough; knead 1 to 2 minutes. Press over bottom and up side of prepared baking sheet; set aside. Prepare Herb Cheese Filling. Spread filling evenly over dough. Let rise in a warm place 30 minutes. Preheat oven to 375°F (190°C). Bake 20 to 30 minutes until crust is golden brown and filling is firm. Cut into 60 to 70 small bars. Serve warm. Makes 60 to 70 appetizer servings.

Herb Cheese Filling:
In a medium bowl, combine all ingredients.

Spicy Wheel

This teenager's delight is almost a pizza, but not quite.

1 envelope active dry yeast
2/3 cup warm water (110°F, 45°C)
1-3/4 to 2 cups all-purpose flour
2 tablespoons vegetable oil
1/2 teaspoon sugar
1/2 teaspoon salt
1 egg, slightly beaten
3 cups grated sharp Cheddar cheese or
   Monterey Jack cheese (12 oz.)

1 (4-oz.) can diced green chilies,
   drained
1 tablespoon chopped pimiento
1/2 teaspoon garlic salt
1 tablespoon minced parsley
About 2 tablespoons milk
2 teaspoons sesame seeds

Grease a 12-inch pizza pan; set aside. In a medium bowl, stir yeast into warm water. Beat in 1 cup flour, oil, sugar and salt. Stir in enough remaining flour to make a medium-stiff dough. Turn out on a lightly floured board. Let rest 3 to 4 minutes. Clean and grease bowl; set aside. Knead dough until smooth and elastic, 5 to 8 minutes. Place in greased bowl, turning once to grease top. Cover and let rise in a warm place about 1 hour until doubled in volume. Punch down dough; divide in half. Cover and let rest 10 minutes. Preheat oven to 400°F (205°C). On a lightly floured board, roll out each piece of dough to a 12-inch circle. Place 1 circle of dough on prepared pizza pan. In a medium bowl, combine egg, cheese, chilies, pimiento, garlic salt and parsley. Spread over dough in pan. Top with other dough circle. Press edges with tines of a fork to seal. Brush top with milk; sprinkle with sesame seeds. Bake 30 to 40 minutes in preheated oven until browned. Cut into narrow wedges; serve warm. Makes 24 to 30 appetizer servings.

Layered French Loaf

Thin baguette loaves make perfect appetizer sandwiches.

1/2 cup chopped ripe olives
1 cup grated sharp Cheddar cheese (4 oz.)
1 cup finely chopped cooked ham
1/2 teaspoon prepared mustard

1/4 cup mayonnaise
1 tablespoon drained sweet pickle relish
1 loaf French bread, about 20" x 2"

In a small bowl, combine olives and cheese; set aside. In a second small bowl, combine ham, mustard, mayonnaise and pickle relish; set aside. Preheat oven to 375°F (190°C). Cut bread lengthwise into 3 equal slices. Spread olive mixture evenly over cut side of bottom slice. Place middle bread slice over olive mixture. Spread ham mixture evenly over middle slice. Top with remaining bread slices, crust-side up. Wrap layered loaf airtight in foil. Bake 15 minutes in pre-heated oven until hot. Cut crosswise into 1-inch slices; serve warm. Makes about 20 appetizer servings.

Spicy Cheese Toast

Create interesting shapes by cutting the bread with small cookie cutters.

3 slices sandwich bread
2 tablespoons butter or margarine
2 tablespoons chutney

1/4 cup grated Cheddar cheese (1 oz.)
Paprika for garnish

Preheat broiler if necessary. Place oven shelf 3 to 6 inches from heating element. Cut crusts from bread; reserve crusts for another use. Cut each bread slice in half. Cut in half again. Arrange on an ungreased baking sheet. In broiler, toast 1 side only. Spread butter or margarine on untoasted side. Finely chop pieces of chutney fruit; spread chutney over butter or margarine. Top evenly with cheese; sprinkle with paprika for garnish. Broil until topping bubbles. Serve hot. Makes about 12 appetizer servings.

Pickled Eggs & Beets

Marinated eggs take on a beautiful beet-red color and spicy pickled flavor.

1 (16-oz.) can sliced beets
6 hard-cooked eggs, peeled
1 cup vinegar
2 tablespoons sugar

1 tablespoon pickling spices
1/2 teaspoon salt
1/8 teaspoon pepper
1 onion, thinly sliced

Drain beets, reserving liquid. Place beets and peeled hard-cooked eggs in a large bowl; set aside. In a medium saucepan, combine beet liquid, vinegar, sugar, pickling spices, salt, pepper and onion. Bring to a boil over medium heat; simmer about 2 minutes. Pour over beets and eggs. Cover and refrigerate 24 hours. Drain and discard marinade. Cut eggs in half lengthwise. Arrange egg halves, beets and onion on a platter or tray. Makes 12 antipasto servings.

Never boil hard-cooked eggs. Whites of boiled eggs are tough and the yolks become dark around the outside.

Herbed Eggs

Herbs flavor the eggs and the marinade gives them a light brown color.

1 cup red wine vinegar
1 cup water
1 teaspoon salt
1/2 teaspoon dried tarragon leaves

1/2 teaspoon dill seeds
1/2 teaspoon ground marjoram
1 garlic clove, crushed
6 hard-cooked eggs, peeled

In a large jar or bowl, combine vinegar, water, salt, tarragon, dill seeds, marjoram and garlic. Add hard-cooked eggs. Spoon mixture over eggs. Cover and refrigerate overnight. Drain and discard marinade. Cut eggs in half lengthwise or cut into wedges. Makes 12 antipasto servings.

How to Make Pickled Eggs & Beets

1/Pour hot beet juice mixture over hard cooked eggs and beets.

2/Cut marinated eggs lengthwise to display color change.

Basic Deviled Eggs

Select your favorite flavor combination from the variations listed below.

6 hard-cooked eggs
3 tablespoons mayonnaise
1/2 teaspoon prepared mustard
2 teaspoons vinegar

1/4 teaspoon salt
1/8 teaspoon pepper
1/8 teaspoon celery seeds, if desired
Chopped parsley for garnish

Cut hard-cooked eggs in half lengthwise. Remove egg yolks; set egg whites aside. In a small bowl, use a fork to mash egg yolks. Stir in mayonnaise, mustard, vinegar, salt, pepper and celery seeds, if desired. Spoon egg yolk mixture evenly into egg white halves. Arrange on a small platter. Garnish with parsley. Makes 12 appetizer servings.

Variations

Curried Chutney Eggs: Cut 6 hard-cooked eggs in half lengthwise. Mash egg yolks; stir in 3 tablespoons mayonnaise, 1 tablespoon finely chopped chutney, 1/2 tcaspoon curry powder and 1/4 teaspoon salt. Spoon evenly into 12 egg white halves.

Caviar Eggs: Cut 6 hard-cooked eggs in half lengthwise. Mash egg yolks; stir in 2 tablespoons melted butter or margarine, 2 tablespoons dairy sour cream, 2 teaspoons lemon juice and 1/4 teaspoon grated onion. Spoon evenly into 12 egg white halves. Sprinkle 1/4 teaspoon caviar on each.

Anchovy Eggs: Cut 6 hard-cooked eggs in half lengthwise. Mash egg yolks; stir in 3 tablespoons melted unsalted butter, 1-1/2 teaspoons anchovy paste, 2 teaspoons lemon juice and 1/8 teaspoon pepper. Spoon evenly into 12 egg white halves.

Fresh Herbed Eggs: Cut 6 hard-cooked eggs in half lengthwise. Mash egg yolks; stir in 3 tablespoons mayonnaise, 2 teaspoons white wine vinegar, 1/2 teaspoon minced tarragon, 2 teaspoons minced watercress, 1 teaspoon minced chives and 1/4 teaspoon salt. Spoon evenly into 12 egg white halves. Garnish each with a watercress sprig.

Rosy Eggs: Cut 6 hard-cooked eggs in half lengthwise. Mash egg yolks; stir in 2 tablespoons dairy sour cream, 4 teaspoons juice from pickled beets, 1/2 teaspoon prepared mustard, 1/4 teaspoon salt and 1/8 teaspoon celery seeds. Spoon evenly into 12 egg white halves.

Bacon & Cheese Eggs: Cut 6 hard-cooked eggs in half lengthwise. Mash egg yolks; stir in 2 slices cooked and finely crumbled bacon, 1/4 cup grated Cheddar cheese, 3 tablespoons mayonnaise, 2 teaspoons vinegar and 1/8 teaspoon salt. Spoon evenly into 12 egg white halves. Garnish with extra bits of crumbled bacon, if desired.

Smoky Deviled Eggs: Cut 6 hard-cooked eggs in half lengthwise. Mash egg yolks; stir in 1 teaspoon prepared mustard, 1/4 cup smoky cheese spread, 1 teaspoon minced parsley, 2 tablespoons milk and 1/8 teaspoon seasoned salt. Spoon evenly into 12 egg white halves. Garnish with parsley sprigs, if desired.

How to Hard-Cook Eggs

Place eggs in a saucepan and cover them with cold water. Bring water to the boiling point but do not boil. Remove from heat; cover and let stand 20 to 25 minutes, or reduce heat and let eggs cook at a very gentle simmer 12 to 15 minutes. Immerse cooked eggs in cold water until no heat remains when you hold an egg in your hand. Tap the shell lightly with the handle of a table knife to crack it. Remove the shell.

Fish & Seafood Catches

Appetizers give us an excuse to enjoy special seafood treats. Begin a festive spring dinner party with something few people will have experienced—Butterflied Shrimp in the shell. The shrimp are cut so they open up slightly when cooked. The piquant sauce flavored with garlic, basil and rosemary adds zest to this delightfully different appetizer. Guests will need small forks to remove the shrimp from their shells.

Because you use small portions in appetizers, feel free to serve shrimp, crabmeat or scallops without upsetting your budget. Plan carefully before making your purchase and use stretchers such as cream cheese, sour cream, eggs and mayonnaise to transform small amounts of seafood into generous appetizer servings.

We prefer the flavor of fresh fish, but frozen and canned are good substitutes in many of these recipes. The meat of fresh fish should be firm to the touch and have a clear color. If the color is cloudy or the edges dry and the aroma strong, the fish has been held too long. Frozen fish should be used soon after thawing to prevent any danger from spoilage. Keep one or more cans of salmon, tuna, sardines and anchovies on your pantry shelf for spontaneous entertaining.

Shrimp is most often associated with appetizers. Fortunately, it is also universally available. Fish markets and large supermarkets usually have shrimp which is uncooked and in the shell. Some markets also have cooked shelled shrimp which is ready to eat. Sometimes you have a choice of different sizes ranging from very tiny bay shrimp to huge prawns. Those most often used for appetizers are very tiny to medium in size. Large or jumbo shrimp are difficult to pick up with your fingers or small wooden picks and are therefore impractical for appetizers.

Crabmeat is also high on the popularity list as an ingredient for appetizers and is available fresh, frozen or canned. If the recipe calls for flaked crabmeat as in Crab Squares and Crab & Swiss on Sourdough, buy less expensive flaked crab instead of whole crab legs.

Butterflied Bayou Shrimp

Have lots of paper napkins ready for guests to shell their own shrimp.

1 lb. medium shrimp in shells, uncooked
1/4 cup butter or margarine
1/4 cup vegetable oil
2 tablespoons lemon juice
1/4 teaspoon salt
1/4 teaspoon pepper
2 tablespoons barbecue sauce

1 bay leaf, crumbled
1 garlic clove, crushed
1/2 teaspoon dried basil leaves
1/2 teaspoon dried rosemary leaves
1/2 teaspoon paprika
1/2 teaspoon crushed dried red peppers

Butterfly shrimp by cutting lengthwise down back, not cutting all the way through. Do not remove shell. In a large skillet, melt butter or margarine; add shrimp. Sauté 3 to 4 minutes until shrimp begin to turn pink. Add remaining ingredients. Simmer over low heat 3 to 4 minutes, stirring occasionally. Cover and let stand about 5 minutes. Spoon shrimp and sauce into a large serving bowl. Makes 35 to 40 appetizer servings.

Shrimp Puffs

Broil these just before they are served.

1 egg white
1/4 to 1/2 teaspoon curry powder
1/4 teaspoon garlic salt

1/2 cup mayonnaise
1 (7-oz.) can shrimp, drained, chopped
30 Melba toast rounds

Preheat broiler if necessary. Place oven rack 5 to 8 inches from heating element. In a medium bowl, beat egg white until stiff but not dry. Stir curry powder and garlic salt into mayonnaise until blended. Fold into beaten egg white. Fold in shrimp. Spoon about 2 teaspoons shrimp mixture evenly over each toast round. Arrange on an ungreased baking sheet or broiler pan. Broil shrimp mixture until bubbly and browned. Serve warm. Makes 30 appetizer servings.

Pickled Shrimp

Furnish wooden or plastic picks or small forks to pick up shrimp.

1 lb. medium shrimp, uncooked
1 tablespoon pickling spices
1 tablespoon Dijon-style mustard
1 teaspoon prepared horseradish
1/4 cup vegetable oil

1/2 teaspoon salt
1/4 teaspoon celery salt
1/2 cup white wine vinegar
2 green onions, sliced

Pull shrimp from shells; discard shells. In a 2-quart saucepan, cover shrimp and pickling spices with water. Bring to a boil; simmer over medium heat about 2 minutes. Strain water, leaving spices on shrimp; set aside. In a small bowl, combine mustard, horseradish, oil, salt, celery salt, vinegar and onions. Pour over drained shrimp. Cover and refrigerate 6 hours or overnight. Serve cold. Makes 35 to 45 appetizer servings.

Potted Shrimp

Cook shrimp only until pink and tender. Overcooking makes them tough.

1/2 lb. shrimp, uncooked	**1/4 teaspoon salt**
1/2 cup butter	**Dash hot pepper sauce**
1 garlic clove, crushed	**1/16 teaspoon ground mace**
1 bay leaf	**1 tablespoon lemon juice**

Remove and discard shrimp shells and veins. Chop shrimp very fine. In a small skillet, melt butter. Add finely chopped shrimp, garlic, bay leaf, salt, hot pepper sauce and mace. Sauté until shrimp is pink and tender, about 4 minutes. Remove and discard bay leaf. Stir lemon juice into shrimp mixture. Spoon into a small bowl or crock. Refrigerate overnight to let flavors blend. Serve cold as a spread. Makes 1-1/2 cups.

Mustard Shrimp

You'll be delighted with the superb flavor.

2 tablespoons prepared mustard	**1/8 teaspoon pepper**
2 tablespoons vinegar	**1/4 cup vegetable oil**
1 tablespoon sugar	**1 teaspoon dried dill weed**
1 egg yolk	**1/2 lb. shelled cooked medium shrimp**
1/4 teaspoon salt	

In a small bowl, beat mustard, vinegar, sugar, egg yolk, salt and pepper. Add oil a little at a time, beating with electric mixer until slightly thickened. Stir in dill weed and shrimp. Cover and refrigerate 6 hours or overnight. Use a slotted spoon to remove shrimp from mustard sauce. Arrange on a small platter; serve cold. Furnish wooden or plastic picks or small forks to pick up shrimp. Makes 20 to 25 appetizer servings.

Smoky Salmon Spread

This delectable smoked salmon flavor drives guests back for seconds and thirds.

1 (3-oz.) pkg. cream cheese, room temperature	**1/8 teaspoon pepper**
1 tablespoon lemon juice	**1/8 teaspoon liquid smoke seasoning**
1/2 teaspoon prepared horseradish	**1 (7-3/4-oz.) can salmon**
1 teaspoon grated onion	**2 tablespoons finely chopped parsley**
1/4 teaspoon salt	**Crackers**

In a medium bowl, combine cream cheese, lemon juice, horseradish, grated onion, salt, pepper and liquid smoke. Thoroughly drain salmon; remove and discard bones. Use 2 forks to flake drained salmon. Stir flaked salmon into cream cheese mixture. Refrigerate about 1 hour. Shape into an 8" x 2-1/2" roll. Sprinkle with parsley; lightly press parsley onto roll. Cut a 12-inch square of plastic wrap or foil. Wrap salmon roll in plastic wrap or foil. Refrigerate 6 hours or overnight. Spread on crackers. Makes about 2 cups.

Buffet Salmon & Cucumber Sauce Photo on page 30.

Guest will exclaim over the beauty and flavor of this exquisite dish.

3 quarts water
1 cup dry white wine
1 carrot, sliced
1 onion, sliced
1 celery stalk, sliced

2 bay leaves
5 whole cloves
1 teaspoon salt
2-1/2 to 3 lbs. cleaned whole salmon
Cucumber Sauce, see below

Cucumber Sauce:
1 small cucumber
1/2 cup dairy sour cream
1/2 cup mayonnaise

1/2 teaspoon dried dill weed
1 tablespoon minced chives
1/4 teaspoon salt

In fish poacher or large roasting pan, combine water, wine, carrot, onion, celery, bay leaves, cloves and salt. Bring to boil, simmer 5 minutes. Cut 3 layers of cheesecloth several inches longer than fish. Place salmon in center of cheesecloth. Holding cheesecloth, carefully lower salmon into pan of boiling wine mixture. Cover and simmer 10 to 15 minutes until salmon flakes easily when pulled apart with a fork. Cool on a rack 15 minutes. Refrigerate salmon in wine mixture 2 to 3 hours or until completely chilled. Prepare Cucumber Sauce; set aside. Holding cheesecloth, lift salmon from pan and place on a large baking sheet with raised sides. For ease in handling, leave fish on cheesecloth until moved to platter. Remove and discard fins and skin. Lift salmon to a large platter; gently remove and discard cheesecloth. Serve cold with Cucumber Sauce. Makes 10 to 12 buffet servings.

Cucumber Sauce:
Peel cucumber; cut in half lengthwise. Scoop out and discard seeds; chop cucumber very fine. In a small bowl, combine chopped cucumber, sour cream, mayonnaise, dill weed, chives and salt.

Bouillabaisse-Style Seafood

Traditional bouillabaisse ingredients flavor this dish.

2 tablespoons olive oil or vegetable oil
1 small onion, chopped
1 garlic clove, crushed
1/4 teaspoon dried basil leaves
1/4 teaspoon pepper
1/4 teaspoon dried marjoram leaves
1/2 teaspoon salt

1 teaspoon lemon juice
Pinch saffron
1 (8-oz.) can tomato sauce
1 cup chicken broth or bouillon
1/2 lb. scallops
1/2 lb. shelled medium shrimp or
    cubed lobster, uncooked

In a large skillet, heat oil. Add onion; sauté until softened. Add garlic, basil, pepper, marjoram, salt, lemon juice, saffron, tomato sauce and broth or bouillon. Simmer uncovered over medium-low heat 10 minutes. If large, cut scallops into 1/2-inch cubes. Add scallops and shrimp or lobster to sauce. Stirring occasionally, cook about 5 minutes until seafood is fork-tender. Turn into a chafing dish or medium, heat-proof bowl on a hot tray. Furnish wooden or plastic picks or small forks to pick up seafood. Makes about 3 cups.

Scallop Puffs

If your scallops are small, cut them into halves instead of quarters.

1/2 lb. large scallops
6 slices sandwich bread
1/4 cup mayonnaise
**2 tablespoons sweet pickle relish,
  drained**

1 tablespoon freshly chopped parsley
1 tablespoon ketchup
1 teaspoon lemon juice
1 egg white

In a medium saucepan, cook scallops in lightly salted water to cover, about 5 minutes. Cut each cooked scallop into 4 pieces; set aside. Remove crusts from bread. Toast bread on 1 side. Cut each slice into 4 squares or triangles. In a small bowl, combine mayonnaise, relish, parsley, ketchup and lemon juice. In a small bowl, beat egg white until stiff but not dry. Fold into mayonnaise mixture. Place 1 piece of cooked scallop on untoasted side of bread. Top with egg white mixture. Preheat broiler if necessary. Place oven shelf 5 to 8 inches from heating element. Arrange unbaked puffs in a broiler pan. Broil puffs 2 to 3 minutes until bubbly and golden brown. Serve hot. Makes 24 appetizer servings.

How to Make Scallop Puffs

1/Cut scallops into pieces smaller than bread squares. Place 1 scallop piece on each square.

2/Spoon about 1 tablespoon egg white mixture over each scallop and bread square.

Skewered Scallops

If your scallops are large, cut them into 3/4-inch pieces for ease in handling.

1 lb. scallops
1 (20-oz.) can chunk-style pineapple
1/4 cup butter or margarine, melted

2 tablespoons finely chopped chutney
1/2 teaspoon curry powder

If scallops are large, cut into quarters or eighths; set aside. Drain pineapple, reserving 2 tablespoons juice. Cut pineapple chunks in half; set aside. Preheat broiler or barbecue grill if necessary. Place oven shelf 5 to 8 inches from heating element. Place a rack in a 15" x 13" broiler pan; set aside. Thread pineapple pieces and scallop pieces alternately on eighteen to twenty-two 4- or 6-inch bamboo skewers. Arrange skewered pieces on rack in broiler pan or on barbecue grill rack; set aside. In a small bowl, combine reserved pineapple juice, butter or margarine, chutney and curry powder. Brush skewered pineapple and scallops with sauce. Broil 3 to 4 minutes until scallops are firm; serve hot. Makes 18 to 22 appetizer servings.

Tiny Tuna Balls

Pick up these crisp tasty tidbits with small wooden or plastic picks.

1 (6-1/2-oz.) can tuna, drained
1 egg, beaten
1/4 cup fine dry breadcrumbs
2 tablespoons mayonnaise

1 tablespoon sweet pickle relish,
** drained**
1/4 teaspoon Worcestershire sauce
1/4 cup vegetable oil

In a medium bowl, flake tuna. Stir in egg, breadcrumbs, mayonnaise, pickle relish and Worcestershire sauce. Shape into 1-inch balls. Heat oil in a large skillet. Fry tuna balls until firm and golden on all sides. Drain on paper towels. Serve warm. Makes 24 appetizer servings.

Herbed Anchovies

Drain the anchovies thoroughly to keep the toast crunchy.

1/4 cup white wine vinegar
1 tablespoon minced chives
1 garlic clove, crushed
1 tablespoon lemon juice
1 tablespoon minced parsley

1/2 teaspoon dried basil leaves,
** crushed**
2 (2-oz.) cans flat anchovy fillets
16 to 18 Melba toast rounds, buttered

In a medium bowl, combine vinegar, chives, garlic, lemon juice, parsley and basil. Drain anchovies. Add drained anchovies to marinade. Cover and refrigerate 6 hours or overnight. To serve, drain anchovies thoroughly. Serve on Melba toast. Makes 16 to 18 appetizer servings.

Sardine Crock

Short processing time leaves bits of onion, sardines and eggs distinguishable.

1 (3-3/4-oz.) can sardines in oil,
  drained
2 hard-cooked eggs, quartered
1/4 cup mayonnaise
1 tablespoon lemon juice

1/2 teaspoon grated onion
1/8 teaspoon salt
1/8 teaspoon pepper
Chopped parsley

In blender or food processor, combine well-drained sardines, eggs, mayonnaise, lemon juice, onion, salt and pepper. Process 5 to 10 seconds until mixed but not pureed. Turn into a small bowl or crock. Sprinkle with parsley. Serve immediately as a spread or refrigerate until ready to serve. Makes about 1 cup.

Hot Crab Dip

Keep warm in a small fondue pot or heat-proof dish on a hot tray.

1 (6-oz.) can crabmeat or
  1 (6-oz.) pkg. frozen crabmeat
1/2 cup dairy sour cream
1 (3-oz.) pkg. cream cheese,
  room temperature
1 tablespoon lemon juice

1 teaspoon prepared horseradish
2 tablespoons minced green pepper
1 tablespoon minced pimiento
French bread, sliced
Potato chips

Drain and flake canned crabmeat or thaw, drain and flake frozen crabmeat; set aside. In a medium saucepan, combine sour cream, cream cheese, lemon juice and horseradish, stirring to blend. Add green pepper, pimiento and flaked crabmeat. Stir over low heat until bubbly. Serve with slices of French bread or potato chips. Makes about 2 cups.

Crab Squares

These morsels are light and puffy with a golden crust.

6 slices sandwich bread
1 (6-oz.) can crabmeat or
  1 (6-oz.) pkg. frozen crabmeat
1/4 cup mayonnaise

1 teaspoon lemon juice
1 teaspoon dried minced onion
1 teaspoon Worcestershire sauce
1 egg white

Remove crusts from bread; lightly toast 1 side. Cut each toasted slice into 4 squares; set aside. Drain and flake canned crabmeat or thaw, drain and flake frozen crabmeat. In a medium bowl, combine flaked crabmeat, mayonnaise, lemon juice, onion and Worcestershire sauce. In a second medium bowl, beat egg white until stiff but not dry. Fold into crabmeat mixture. Spoon about 2 teaspoons on untoasted side of each toast square. Preheat broiler if necessary. Place oven shelf 5 to 8 inches from heating element. Arrange toast squares in a broiler pan or on a large baking sheet. Broil 4 to 5 minutes until browned and bubbly. Makes 24 appetizer servings.

Crab & Swiss on Sourdough

When using frozen crabmeat, allow thawing time.

1 (6-oz.) can crabmeat or
   1 (6-oz.) pkg. frozen crabmeat
1 cup grated Swiss cheese (4 oz.)
1/2 cup dairy sour cream
2 tablespoons minced green onions
1 tablespoon lemon juice

1/2 teaspoon Worcestershire sauce
1/4 teaspoon salt
1 (8-1/2-oz.) can water chestnuts,
   drained
3 (6- or 7-inch) sourdough rolls

Drain and flake canned crabmeat or thaw, drain and flake frozen crabmeat. In a small bowl, combine flaked crabmeat, cheese, sour cream, onions, lemon juice, Worcestershire sauce and salt; set aside. Slice 10 water chestnuts into thirds; set aside. Finely chop remaining water chestnuts; add to crabmeat mixture. Preheat oven to 400°F (205°C). Slice each sourdough roll into 10 crosswise slices. Spoon about 2 teaspoons crabmeat mixture evenly onto each slice. Top each with 1 slice water chestnut. Arrange on an ungreased baking sheet. Bake 10 to 15 minutes until bubbly and slightly browned. Serve hot. Makes 30 appetizer servings.

How to Make Crab & Swiss on Sourdough

1/Cut each sourdough roll into 10 crosswise slices. Cut smaller rolls into 6 or 7 slices.

2/Spoon about 3 tablespoons filling on each bread slice; top with slice of water chestnut.

Poultry Pick-Ups

Take a world flavor tour with us as you sample Chicken Dijon Tidbits and imagine you're in France. Or savor the spiciness of Chicken Sate and dream of Singapore. Tahitian Sunset Roll-Ups with a touch of curry accented with coconut and peanuts will remind you of waving palms and splashing surf.

The moderate cost of poultry has made it a favorite appetizer food. It is not only one of the lowest priced meats available, but is exceptionally rich in protein. You can buy poultry by the piece, boned, rolled, all white meat, all dark meat and by the whole bird.

Most chicken appetizers are made from the tender breasts of young fryers, roasters or broilers. If convenience is important to you, buy boned chicken breasts. They save time and are easy to cut into cubes. To stretch your budget,

buy chicken parts or a whole chicken and bone it yourself. Before cutting, partially freeze the boned meat. This makes it easier to cut into small pieces. Cook fresh poultry a very short time. Long cooking makes it tough and stringy.

Holiday meals which include turkey generally have leftovers which can be utilized in appetizer dishes. Cut large pieces into small cubes and thread on bamboo skewers for Turkey Brochettes. Apricot jam and ketchup are combined with hot pepper sauce to make an interesting and zingy sauce sure to please guests. Chicken can be used, but pieces will be smaller and not as uniform in size. Grind bits and pieces of meat to make Turkey Rounds. Broil until crispy, then serve plain or dip these small turkey meatballs into the warm orange sauce included with Orange & Honey Meatballs.

Chicken Sate

You can also make this with lean boneless pork cubes.

2 tablespoons vegetable oil	**1 cup chicken broth or bouillon**
1 garlic clove, crushed	**1/2 teaspoon salt**
1 tomato, peeled, seeded, chopped	**1/2 teaspoon crushed dried red pepper**
1/4 cup chunk-style peanut butter	**1 lb. boneless chicken breasts**

In a small skillet, heat oil and garlic. Stir in tomato, peanut butter, broth or bouillon, salt and red pepper. Simmer about 10 minutes, stirring occasionally; set aside to cool. Remove skin from chicken breasts; cut into 3/4- to 1-inch pieces. Thread 3 or 4 pieces on each of twelve to sixteen 4-inch bamboo skewers. Arrange in a 12" x 7" baking pan. Pour peanut butter marinade over skewered chicken; cover and refrigerate 5 to 6 hours. Preheat broiler if necessary. Place oven shelf 3 to 4 inches from heating element. Broil in oven or on barbecue grill until browned. Brush with marinade; turn and broil other side until browned and tender. Serve hot. Makes 12 to 16 appetizer servings.

Chicken Dijon Tidbits

These skewered chicken tidbits have a superb flavor.

2 whole chicken breasts, skinned, boned
1/4 cup butter or margarine
2 teaspoons Dijon-style mustard
1 garlic clove, crushed
1 tablespoon minced parsley

1 teaspoon lemon juice
1/8 teaspoon salt
1/4 cup fine dry breadcrumbs
1/4 cup grated Parmesan cheese (1 oz.)

Cut chicken breasts into 3/4-inch cubes. In a medium skillet, melt butter or margarine. Stir in mustard, garlic, parsley, lemon juice and salt. Add chicken; sauté over medium heat 5 to 10 minutes, turning chicken until lightly browned on all sides. Sprinkle with breadcrumbs and Parmesan cheese. Toss until chicken is evenly coated. Spoon into a flat serving dish. Serve warm. Pick up individual pieces with small wooden or plastic picks. Makes 70 to 75 appetizer servings.

Orange & Honey Meatballs

Dip these little meatballs into this spicy orange sauce for a flavor surprise.

3 cups chopped cooked chicken
1 (8-oz.) can water chestnuts, drained
2 green onions, chopped
1 egg, beaten
1/2 teaspoon salt
1/8 teaspoon pepper
1/4 cup butter or margarine

1 tablespoon cornstarch
1 cup orange juice
1/8 teaspoon ground allspice
2 tablespoons honey
2 tablespoons dry white wine
1 tablespoon soy sauce

In blender or food processor, combine chicken, water chestnuts, onions, egg, salt and pepper. Process until finely chopped. Preheat oven to 375°F (190°C). Shape chicken mixture into 1-inch balls. Arrange on an ungreased baking sheet with raised sides. Bake 15 to 20 minutes in preheated oven or until firm. In a small saucepan, melt butter or margarine. In a small bowl, stir cornstarch into orange juice until dissolve; stir into melted butter or margarine. Stir in allspice, honey, wine and soy sauce. Cook and stir over low heat until slightly thickened and translucent. To serve, dip warm meatballs into warm sauce. Makes about 60 appetizer servings.

Buy a larger chicken or turkey than needed for one meal. Cut extra cooked poultry into small cubes and use it in appetizers.

Chicken Wing Drumsticks

This budget-stretcher will be a favorite with your guests.

12 chicken wings
1/3 cup sesame seeds
2/3 cup fine dry breadcrumbs
1/2 teaspoon paprika

1/2 teaspoon salt
1/2 teaspoon seasoned salt
1/2 cup half-and-half
1/4 cup butter or margarine, melted

Remove and discard wing tips. Separate remaining wing sections. Cut skin at small end of each wing section. Pull out one of the bones from section having 2 bones; set aside. Preheat oven to 350°F (175°C). In a small skillet, toast sesame seeds over low heat until golden, stirring occasionally. In a small shallow bowl, combine toasted sesame seeds, breadcrumbs, paprika, salt and seasoned salt. Dip wing sections into half-and-half, then into breadcrumb mixture. Arrange in a 13" x 9" baking pan. Pour melted butter or margarine over chicken. Bake 45 to 55 minutes in preheated oven until tender. Makes 24 appetizer servings.

Chicken & Almond Turnovers

Serve these baked turnovers warm or cold.

1 tablespoon butter or margarine
1/4 cup chopped onion
1 garlic clove, minced
1/2 chicken breast, boned, chopped
4 cherry tomatoes, seeded, chopped
1/4 teaspoon curry powder
1/8 teaspoon dried basil leaves,
  crumbled

1/8 teaspoon salt
1 tablespoon finely chopped
  blanched almonds
Appetizer Pastry, page 75 or
  pie dough of choice

In a medium skillet, melt butter or margarine; add onion, garlic, and chicken. Cook and stir over medium heat about 5 minutes. Stir in tomatoes, curry powder, basil and salt. Simmer over medium heat until flavors blend, about 5 minutes. Stir in almonds; set aside to cool slightly. Preheat oven to 400°F (205°C). Prepare pastry dough; roll out 1/8-inch thick on a lightly floured board. Cut pastry into 3-inch circles. Place 1-1/2 teaspoons chicken mixture on 1 side of each circle. Fold other half of circle over chicken mixture. Press edges with tines of a fork to seal. Arrange on an ungreased baking sheet or in a 13" x 9" baking pan. Bake about 15 minutes in preheated oven until browned. Makes 20 to 22 appetizer servings.

Boil or poach chicken breasts or thighs in chicken broth. Cool in the broth for greater flavor and a moist texture.

Tahitian Sunset Roll-Ups

Emerald morsels that are sure to please.

2 whole chicken breasts, cut in half
2 cups chicken broth or bouillon
4 teaspoons curry powder

24 to 32 small lettuce leaves
Tahitian Dip, see below
1 cup toasted coconut

Tahitian Dip:
1 cup dairy sour cream
2 tablespoons finely chopped peanuts

1/4 cup finely chopped chutney

In a medium saucepan, combine chicken breasts, broth or bouillon and curry powder. Bring to a boil; simmer about 25 minutes or until chicken is tender. Refrigerate chicken in broth until cool. Remove chicken breasts from broth. Remove and discard skin and bones. Cut each half breast into 6 to 8 lengthwise strips. Place each strip of chicken across one side of each lettuce leaf. Fold ends of lettuce over chicken; roll up. Secure with a wooden pick if necessary. Refrigerate at least 1 hour. Prepare Tahitian Dip. Spoon coconut into a small bowl. On a tray or large platter, arrange lettuce-wrapped chicken around dip and coconut. To serve, dip chicken rolls into Tahitian Dip then into coconut. Makes 24 to 32 appetizer servings.

Tatitian Dip:
In a small bowl, combine, sour cream, peanuts and chutney.

Chicken Paste

Makes a great topping for crackers or Melba toast.

2 tablespoons butter or margarine
1/2 cup chopped blanched almonds
1 whole chicken breast, cooked
1 tablespoon chopped parsley
1/8 teaspoon salt

1/8 teaspoon pepper
2 tablespoons vegetable oil
3 tablespoons dry white wine
2 tablespoons whipping cream

In a small skillet, melt butter or margarine. Add almonds; sauté until golden brown. Set aside to cool. Remove and discard bones and skin from chicken breast; chop meat. In blender or food processor, combine chopped chicken, sautéed almonds, parsley, salt, pepper, oil, wine and cream. Process until almost smooth. Makes 1-1/4 cups.

How to Make Tahitian Sunset Roll-Ups

1/For a golden color, cool cooked chicken breasts in curried broth. Cut cold breasts into lengthwise strips.

2/Fold sides of lettuce leaf over ends of chicken then roll up. Secure lettuce leaf with a wooden pick.

Turkey Brochettes

Cut turkey into larger pieces if you prefer a more hearty snack.

**2 cups cubed cooked turkey
  (1/2- to 3/4-inch cubes)**
1/4 cup vegetable oil
1/4 cup apricot jam
1/2 cup ketchup

1 teaspoon grated onion
1 teaspoon Worcestershire sauce
1/4 teaspoon salt
3 to 4 drops hot pepper sauce

Cut cooked turkey into 1/2- to 3/4-inch cubes. Thread 3 or 4 cubes turkey on each of twelve to fifteen 4-inch bamboo skewers. Place in a 12" x 7" baking dish; set aside. In a small bowl, combine oil, jam, ketchup, onion, Worcestershire sauce, salt and hot pepper sauce. Pour over skewered turkey pieces. Cover and refrigerate 6 hours or overnight to blend flavors. Drain, reserving sauce. Preheat broiler if necessary. Place oven shelf 3 to 4 inches from heating element. Broil in oven or on barbecue grill until browned and crisp on edges. Brush with sauce; turn and brown other side. Makes 12 to 15 appetizer servings.

Turkey Cubes   Photo on pages 2 and 3.

Use spicy barbecue sauce if you want a pronounced flavor.

1 (8-oz.) can jellied cranberry sauce
1/2 cup barbecue sauce
1/8 teaspoon ground allspice

1/2 teaspoon grated orange peel
3 cups cubed cooked turkey
   (1-inch cubes)

In a chafing dish, heat cranberry sauce, barbecue sauce, allspice and orange peel, stirring to blend. Stir in cubed turkey; heat 10 minutes. Serve warm. Pick up individual pieces with small wooden or plastic picks. Makes 3 cups or about 45 appetizer servings.

Turkey Rounds

Use yesterday's turkey to make these savory appetizers.

1/4 cup butter, melted
1/8 teaspoon paprika
2 cups ground cooked turkey
1/4 cup mayonnaise
1 teaspoon dried minced onion

1 egg, beaten
1/2 cup soft breadcrumbs
1/4 cup minced celery
1/2 teaspoon salt
1/8 teaspoon pepper

In a small bowl, combine butter and paprika; set aside. Preheat oven to 400°F (205°C). In a medium bowl, combine turkey, mayonnaise, onion, egg, breadcrumbs, celery, salt and pepper. Shape into 1-inch balls. Roll in butter mixture. Arrange in a 13'' x 9'' baking pan. Bake 10 to 15 minutes in preheated oven until browned and firm. Makes 30 to 35 appetizer servings.

Curried Turkey Spread

Save time by heating the spread in a non-metal bowl in your microwave oven.

2 cups cubed cooked turkey or chicken
   (1/2- to 1-inch cubes)
1 small apple, peeled, cored, diced
1 teaspoon chopped chives
1/2 cup butter, cut in 6 to 8 pieces

1/2 teaspoon curry powder
1 teaspoon lemon juice
1/2 teaspoon salt
1/8 teaspoon pepper
Crackers or Melba toast

In food processor, combine turkey or chicken, apple and chives. Turning machine on and off several times, cut with metal blade until finely chopped. Add butter, curry powder, lemon juice, salt and pepper. Turn machine on and off several times until mixture is smooth. Spoon into a small saucepan and stir over medium heat until warmed, 3 to 5 minutes. Serve warm with crackers or Melba toast. Makes 2-1/4 cups.

Vegetables

Flavor, texture, color and versatility as well as their low calorie content make vegetables popular appetizer foods. Raw vegetables can be chopped, stuffed, cut in rounds, marinated or combined with meats or cheese. Cut into flowers or whimsical shapes, they become edible garnishes or center pieces. Bake them in quiches or combine with other vegetables or cheeses in dips.

Possibilities for vegetable appetizers are almost limitless. We combined eggplant with tomatoes, green pepper, onion, carrot and other vegetables to make an array of delicious appetizers. Use the total vegetable when possible. The scooped-out shell of a fresh eggplant makes an attractive container for an eggplant dip. Surround it with chunks of pita bread or Armenian cracker bread and you've brought an Eastern Mediterranean flavor to your party. You'll enjoy Eggplant Caviar and Cheese Caponata. They are spicy, good tasting and attractive.

Marinated vegetables are easy to prepare and are excellent when served at buffets. Cold, crisp, tangy vegetables provide texture and flavor contrast when served with a plate of sliced meat and cheese. Marinated carrots, cucumbers, broccoli and beans also add colorful accents. Prepare marinated vegetables the day before your party to allow flavors to blend and to eliminate last minute preparations. For a dramatic display, arrange and serve them in your prettiest glass bowls.

You may not think of jelly as an appetizer, but we feel this is where our exotic Jalapeno Pepper Jelly belongs. If your guests enjoy hot peppers, this will be a favorite. Spread crackers with cream cheese, then top with a small amount of jelly. The pungent taste is magnificent.

Plan an Antipasto Platter

Mix or match any of these vegetable appetizers with a tray of sliced cold meats, cheese, anchovies and tuna:

Venetian Crowns

Sliced stuffed olives provide an interesting garnish.

2 (6-oz.) jars marinated artichoke crowns
  or bottoms, drained
1 egg, beaten
1/4 cup grated Parmesan cheese (1 oz.)

1/2 cup ricotta cheese
10 slices pepperoni sausage
2 tablespoons fine dry breadcrumbs
10 stuffed olives, sliced

Preheat oven to 325°F (165°C). Grease a 13'' x 9'' baking dish. Arrange artichoke crowns or bottoms over bottom of dish. In a small bowl, combine egg, Parmesan cheese and ricotta cheese. Finely chop pepperoni slices; add to cheese mixture. Spoon into centers of artichoke crowns or bottoms. Sprinkle with breadcrumbs. Bake 20 minutes in preheated oven until cheeses melt. Garnish with olive slices. Serve hot. Makes 20 to 22 appetizer servings.

Monterey Artichoke Bake

Marinade on the artichokes has a tangy flavor.

2 (6-oz.) jars marinated artichoke hearts
1 small onion, finely chopped
1 garlic clove, crushed
4 eggs
1/4 cup fine dry breadcrumbs
2 cups grated Monterey Jack cheese
  (8 oz.)
1/4 teaspoon salt

1/4 teaspoon dried basil leaves, crushed
1/4 teaspoon dried oregano leaves,
  crushed
1/8 teaspoon pepper
2 tablespoons finely chopped canned
  green chilies
Pimiento strips, if desired

Drain artichoke hearts, reserving 1 tablespoon marinade in a small saucepan. Set artichoke hearts aside. Add onion and garlic to reserved marinade. Sauté until onions are soft. Preheat oven to 325°F (165°C). Grease an 8-inch square baking pan; set aside. Finely chop artichoke hearts; set aside. In a medium bowl, beat eggs until foamy. Stir in chopped artichoke hearts, breadcrumbs, Monterey Jack cheese, salt, basil, oregano, pepper, green chilies and sautéed onion mixture. Spoon into prepared baking pan. Bake 25 to 30 minutes in preheated oven until mixture is firm. Cut into 25 to 30 small bars or squares. Garnish each piece with a strip of pimiento, if desired. Serve warm or cold. Makes 25 to 30 appetizer servings.

Hot Chokes

Hot *refers to the temperature, not the taste.*

1 (6-oz.) jar marinated artichoke hearts
1 cup mayonnaise
1 cup grated Parmesan cheese (4 oz.)

40 to 45 Melba toast rounds
40 to 45 pimiento strips

Drain artichoke hearts; finely chop. In a medium bowl, combine chopped artichoke hearts, mayonnaise and Parmesan cheese. Arrange Melba toast rounds on 2 ungreased baking sheets. Preheat broiler if necessary. Place oven rack 5 to 8 inches from heating element. Spoon about 2 teaspoons cheese mixture on each round. Broil until topping bubbles, about 1 minute. Garnish each with 1 strip of pimiento; serve warm. Makes 40 to 45 appetizer servings.

Curried Artichoke Leaves

Mild-flavored artichoke leaves and heart pieces are used as dippers.

1 large artichoke
1/4 lb. shelled cooked shrimp
1/2 cup mayonnaise

1/8 teaspoon garlic salt
1/2 teaspoon curry powder
1/8 teaspoon paprika

Cut or break stem from artichoke. Use scissors to trim points from all leaves. In a large pot or Dutch oven, pour lightly salted water to cover artichoke. Over medium heat, cook until leaves can be pulled out easily, about 30 minutes; drain. Pull out and reserve leaves. Cut out and discard choke. Chop artichoke heart into 1/2-inch pieces. Insert a wooden pick into each piece; set aside. Chop shrimp very fine. In a small bowl, combine chopped shrimp, mayonnaise, garlic salt, curry powder and paprika. Place bowl in center of a large plate. Surround bowl with cooked artichoke leaves and pieces of artichoke heart. To serve, dip leaves and hearts into shrimp mixture. Makes about 50 appetizer servings.

Dilled Beans & Carrots

These will add color to your cocktail buffet table or antipasto tray.

4 medium carrots (about 3/4 lb.)
10 to 16 oz. fresh or frozen green beans
2 cups white vinegar
1/4 cup honey
1 teaspoon dried dill weed

1 teaspoon pickling spices
1 garlic clove, crushed
1/2 cup water
1 tablespoon salt

Peel carrots; cut into sticks. If using fresh beans, remove ends; break in half. Thaw frozen beans. In a large saucepan, combine vinegar, honey, dill weed, pickling spices, garlic, water and salt. Bring to a boil over high heat. Carefully lower carrot sticks and broken beans into boiling mixture. Cover and simmer 10 minutes over low heat. Set aside to cool 10 minutes. Refrigerate 3 to 4 hours. Spoon into a large serving dish. Makes about 10 buffet servings.

Marinated Garbanzo Beans

For a special treat, serve with sliced salami or pepperoni.

1/2 cup vegetable oil
1/2 cup red wine vinegar
1/4 teaspoon garlic salt
1/2 teaspoon fines herbes
2 tablespoons minced parsley

2 tablespoons minced chives
1/4 teaspoon salt
1/8 teaspoon pepper
2 (15-oz.) cans garbanzo beans, drained

In a medium bowl, combine oil, vinegar, garlic salt, fines herbes, parsley, chives, salt and pepper, stirring to blend. Stir in drained beans. Cover and refrigerate 6 hours or overnight. Drain; arrange on an antipasto tray. Makes 4 cups.

Stuffed Cucumber Slices

These are especially attractive on a Christmas appetizer tray.

1 large cucumber
1 (3-oz.) pkg. cream cheese,
  room temperature
1 tablespoon blue cheese, crumbled

1 teaspoon grated onion
2 teaspoons minced parsley
1/2 teaspoon dried dill weed
20 to 25 pimiento strips

Score cucumber by pressing tines of a fork about 1/16-inch into peel at one end and pulling tines lengthwise leaving grooves. Turn cucumber and continue scoring until grooves are lengthwise over entire surface. Cut 1-inch slice from 1 end. Use an iced tea spoon to scoop seeds from inside cucumber. Stand on cut end on paper towels to drain, about 10 minutes. In a small bowl, combine cream cheese, blue cheese, onion, parsley and dill weed. Spoon mixture into hollowed-out center of cucumber. Wrap in foil or plastic wrap; refrigerate 3 to 4 hours. Slice crosswise into 1/4-inch slices. Garnish slices with pimiento strips. Makes 20 to 25 slices.

Stuffed Brussels Sprouts

A rare blend—good nutrition and excellent taste!

1-1/2 to 2 lbs. brussels sprouts
1 cup Italian salad dressing
1/2 cup cottage cheese

1/2 teaspoon grated onion
1 (2-oz.) pkg. blue cheese, crumbled
1/2 teaspoon seasoned salt

In a medium saucepan, pour lightly salted water to cover brussels sprouts. Cook over medium heat until crisp-tender, about 15 minutes; drain. With a small melon ball cutter or knife, remove center core from each cooked sprout. Reserve centers for another use. Place shells cut-side down on paper towels to drain thoroughly, about 15 minutes. Place drained sprouts in a medium bowl; pour salad dressing evenly over each sprout. Cover and refrigerate 6 hours or overnight; drain. In a small bowl, combine cottage cheese, grated onion, blue cheese and seasoned salt. Spoon cheese mixture evenly into drained sprouts. Makes about 40 appetizer servings.

How to Make Stuffed Cucumber Slices

1/Cut a 1-inch slice from one end of scored cucumber. Use an iced tea spoon to scoop seeds from inside.

2/Cut chilled, stuffed cucumber in 1/4-inch slices. Garnish with slivers of pimiento.

Marinated Vegetables

Add other vegetables that appeal to you. A great way to eat leftovers.

2 cups white wine vinegar
2/3 cup vegetable oil
1 garlic clove, crushed
1 teaspoon dry mustard
1 teaspoon dried tarragon leaves,
  crushed
1/2 teaspoon salt

12 peppercorns
2 tablespoons sugar
2 carrots, peeled, cut in sticks
1 large cucumber, sliced
2 zucchini, sliced
1 onion, sliced

In a large bowl, combine vinegar, oil, garlic, mustard, tarragon, salt, peppercorns and sugar; stir to blend. Add carrots, cucumber, zucchini and onion. Cover and marinate at least 8 hours. Drain and serve. Makes 8 to 10 antipasto servings.

Spiced Carrot Sticks   Photo on pages 2 and 3.

For variety, cut the carrots in thin diagonal slices or traditional round slices.

5 large carrots (about 1 lb.)
1 cup white wine vinegar
1/2 cup orange juice

1/4 cup honey
1 tablespoon pickling spices

Peel carrots; cut into thin sticks. In a medium saucepan, combine vinegar, orange juice, honey and pickling spices. Add carrot sticks. Bring to a boil. Simmer over medium-low heat 8 to 10 minutes until carrots are crisp-tender. Cool on a rack 15 minutes. Pour carrots and sauce into a medium bowl with a tight-fitting lid. Cover and refrigerate 6 hours or overnight. Drain to serve. Makes 8 to 10 appetizer servings.

Wrapped Celery Chunks

For the best results, use very thinly sliced meat.

10 (4-inch) celery stalks
1 (5-oz.) jar pineapple cream cheese

1 (2-1/2-oz.) pkg. very thinly sliced
   spiced beef or turkey

Fill celery stalks with cream cheese. Wrap each filled stalk in a slice of beef or turkey. Place seam-side down on a small platter. Refrigerate at least 1 hour. Cut each stalk into 3 or 4 pieces. Secure meat with a wooden pick if necessary. Makes 30 to 40 appetizer servings.

Eggplant Caviar

If you like vegetables, this one will be a favorite.

2 medium tomatoes
1/4 cup vegetable oil
2 medium onions, finely chopped
1 green pepper, finely chopped
1 eggplant, peeled, finely chopped

1 teaspoon salt
1/4 teaspoon pepper
1 teaspoon sugar
1 teaspoon vinegar
Toast or crackers

Peel, seed and finely chop tomatoes. Place in a strainer; let drain about 10 minutes. In a large skillet, heat oil. Add onions; sauté 2 to 3 minutes until tender. Stir in green pepper and eggplant. Sauté 2 to 3 minutes longer. Add drained tomatoes, salt, pepper, sugar and vinegar. Simmer 15 to 20 minutes to blend flavors. Refrigerate at least 2 hours. Serve cold with toast or crackers. Makes about 3-1/2 cups.

Sicilian Squares

Eggplant is so well disguised in this dish even vegetable-haters will like it.

1 medium eggplant
2 eggs, slightly beaten
1/2 cup soft breadcrumbs
1 teaspoon lemon juice
1/2 teaspoon salt
1/4 teaspoon pepper

1 garlic clove, crushed
1/2 teaspoon chili powder
1 cup grated sharp Cheddar cheese (4 oz.)
2 tablespoons grated Parmesan cheese or
   Romano cheese

In a large saucepan with a tight-fitting lid, steam unpeeled eggplant in steamer basket over 1 to 2 inches boiling water until tender, about 20 minutes. Or cook in microwave oven according to manufacturer's directions until tender. Peel and mash cooked eggplant. Grease an 8-inch square pan; set aside. Preheat oven to 350°F (175°C). Combine mashed eggplant, eggs, breadcrumbs, lemon juice, salt, pepper, garlic, chili powder and Cheddar cheese. Spoon into prepared pan. Sprinkle top with Parmesan cheese or Romano cheese. Bake 25 to 30 minutes in preheated oven until firm in center. Cut into 2-inch squares; serve warm. Makes 16 appetizer servings.

Cheese Caponata

This spicy variation of eggplant caviar is excellent cold but tastier when served warm.

1/4 cup vegetable oil
1 small eggplant, peeled, diced
2 medium tomatoes, peeled, seeded, diced
1 small onion, diced
1/2 teaspoon salt
1/8 teaspoon pepper
2 tablespoons red wine vinegar

1 garlic clove, crushed
1 teaspoon prepared mustard
1/4 cup finely chopped ripe olives
1 cup ricotta cheese
French bread, cut or torn in large pieces,
   or pumpernickel bread, thinly sliced

In a large skillet, heat oil. Add eggplant; sauté 3 to 4 minutes until limp. Add tomatoes, onion, salt, pepper, vinegar and garlic. Simmer uncovered about 5 minutes until mixture is thick but not dry. Stir in mustard, olives and ricotta cheese. Serve warm or cold. Use as a spread on French bread or pumpernickel bread. Makes 3 cups.

Crush garlic by placing the peeled garlic clove in the bowl of a large spoon. Press firmly with the back of another large spoon.

Stuffed Eggplant Dip

The unbaked eggplant shell makes a container for the vegetable dip.

1 large eggplant
1 tablespoon lemon juice
1/4 cup olive oil or vegetable oil
1 green pepper, seeded, diced
2 celery stalks, diced
1 onion, diced
1 carrot, finely chopped
1 garlic clove, crushed

1 tablespoon red wine vinegar
2 tomatoes, peeled, seeded, chopped
2 tablespoons chopped cilantro leaves
1/4 teaspoon dried basil leaves
1 teaspoon salt
1/8 teaspoon cayenne pepper
Pita bread or sourdough bread

Cut eggplant in half lengthwise. Use a spoon to scoop out pulp, leaving a 1/2-inch shell; reserve pulp. Brush inside of eggplant shells with lemon juice to prevent browning; set aside. In a medium saucepan, steam or cook reserved pulp in boiling water until tender, about 8 minutes; set aside. In a large skillet, heat oil. Add green pepper, celery, onion and carrot. Sauté until vegetables are tender, 3 to 4 minutes. Stir in garlic, vinegar, tomatoes, cilantro, basil, salt, cayenne pepper and cooked eggplant pulp. Stirring occasionally, cook over medium heat 10 to 15 minutes or until vegetables are very tender. Cut pita bread or sourdough bread into wedges; set aside. Spoon cooked vegetable mixture into eggplant shells. Serve warm or refrigerate 1 hour and serve as a dip with pita bread or sourdough bread. Makes 3-1/2 cups.

Moroccan Eggplant Appetizer

Scoop up this mixture with pieces of pita bread.

1 large eggplant, peeled
2/3 cup olive oil or vegetable oil
1 medium zucchini, diced
1 garlic clove, crushed
1 onion, chopped
1 (14-1/2-oz.) can Italian-style
   tomatoes, chopped
1/4 cup sliced pimiento-stuffed
   green olives

2 tablespoons capers
1 tablespoon red wine vinegar
1 teaspoon sugar
1 teaspoon salt
2 tablespoons chopped parsley
1/2 teaspoon fines herbes
1/4 teaspoon pepper
Pita bread or French bread

Cut eggplant into 1/2-inch cubes. In a large skillet, heat oil. Add eggplant; sauté until soft, 3 to 4 minutes. Stir in zucchini, garlic, onion, tomatoes, olives, capers, vinegar, sugar, salt, parsley, fines herbes and pepper. Stirring occasionally, cook over medium heat until vegetables are very soft and most of liquid evaporates, about 20 minutes; cool on a rack. Spoon into a medium serving bowl. To serve, dip pieces of pita bread or French bread into mixture. Makes about 4 cups.

Stir & Serve Mushrooms

Prepare the sauce ahead of time and you'll have hot hors d'oeuvres almost instantly.

3/4 lb. small mushrooms
1/4 cup butter or margarine
2 anchovy fillets, mashed
1 garlic clove, crushed

2 tablespoons minced parsley
1 tablespoon Worcestershire sauce
1/8 teaspoon pepper

Wipe mushrooms with a damp cloth; set aside. In a large skillet, melt butter or margarine. Add mushrooms. Stirring constantly with a wooden spoon, sauté over medium heat about 1 minute. In a small bowl, combine anchovies, garlic, parsley, Worcestershire sauce and pepper. Stir into mushrooms. Cook and stir over low heat until mixture is hot, about 2 minutes. Serve warm. Makes 35 to 40 appetizer servings.

Greek-Style Mushrooms

Fennel seeds give the mushrooms a very slight licorice flavor.

1 lb. small mushrooms
1/2 cup olive oil or vegetable oil
1/4 cup dry white wine
2 tablespoons lemon juice
1/2 cup water
1 garlic clove, crushed

1 teaspoon salt
1/4 teaspoon pepper
1 teaspoon sugar
1/4 teaspoon fennel seeds
1/2 teaspoon ground coriander

Wipe mushrooms with a damp cloth. Set aside in a large heat-proof bowl. In a small saucepan, combine remaining ingredients. Bring to boil over medium heat; simmer about 2 minutes. Immediately, pour over mushrooms. Cover and cool to room temperature. Refrigerate 6 hours or overnight. Serve with wooden picks. Makes 65 to 70 appetizer servings.

Marinated Mushrooms

Let your guests spear the mushrooms with wooden picks.

1 lb. small mushrooms
1/2 cup vegetable oil
1/2 cup red wine vinegar
1 garlic clove, crushed
1/2 teaspoon dried oregano leaves

1/2 teaspoon dried thyme leaves
1/4 teaspoon pepper
1/4 teaspoon paprika
1/2 teaspoon salt
1 small onion, thinly sliced

Wipe mushrooms with a damp cloth. In a medium saucepan, steam or cook in boiling water 1 minute. Drain and quickly cover with cold water; immediately drain again. In a large bowl, combine oil, vinegar, garlic, oregano, thyme, pepper, paprika and salt, stirring to blend. Stir in onion slices and drained mushrooms. Cover and refrigerate at least 24 hours. Makes about 4 cups.

Oyster-Stuffed Mushrooms

If you make these ahead and refrigerate them, add water to the pan just before baking.

1 (3-2/3-oz.) can smoked oysters
1 lb. medium mushrooms
2 tablespoons minced green onions

1/2 cup dairy sour cream
1/2 cup fine dry breadcrumbs

Turn oysters into a strainer; set aside to drain. Wipe mushrooms with a damp cloth; remove stems. Chop mushroom stems very fine. In a medium bowl, combine chopped mushroom stems, onions, sour cream and breadcrumbs. Chop drained oysters very fine. Add to breadcrumb mixture. Preheat oven to 375°F (190°C). Spoon oyster mixture evenly into mushroom caps. Arrange filled mushrooms over bottom of a 13" x 9" baking dish, filling-side up. Pour 1/2 cup water around but not on mushrooms. Bake 15 to 20 minutes in preheated oven until mushrooms are tender. Serve warm. Makes 40 to 50 appetizer servings.

Stuffed Grape Leaves

Buy bottled grape leaves in gourmet food stores or ethnic sections of supermarkets.

1 (8-oz.) jar grape leaves in brine
1/4 cup olive oil or vegetable oil
1 onion, chopped
1/2 cup rice, uncooked
2 tablespoons pine nuts
1 cup chicken broth or bouillon
1/4 cup chopped parsley

1/2 teaspoon salt
1/8 teaspoon pepper
1 tablespoon lemon juice
1/8 teaspoon ground allspice
2 tablespoons dried currants
Hot water
Lemon slices for garnish

Gently separate leaves; rinse in warm water. Select 35 to 40 full leaves without tears; reserve remaining leaves. Cut stems from selected leaves; set aside. Heat oil in a medium skillet. Add onion; sauté until softened. Add rice and pine nuts; sauté until lightly browned. Stir in broth or bouillon, parsley, salt, pepper, lemon juice and allspice. Cover and simmer over low heat 15 minutes. Stir in currants; set stuffing aside. Place a metal rack in bottom of a large kettle or Dutch oven. Make a bed of imperfect reserved leaves on rack. Place trimmed leaves on a flat surface, vein side up and stem-end toward you. Spoon 1-1/2 to 2 tablespoons stuffing on stem-end of each. Fold right and left sides over stuffing and roll up as tightly as possible jelly-roll fashion. Stack stuffed leaves very close together over bed of leaves. Place a heavy plate or dish on top of stuffed grape leaves to hold rolls in place. Add hot water to cover. Cover and simmer over low heat 45 to 50 minutes. Remove cooked rolls from water; set aside to cool. Discard water. Arrange cooked rolls on a platter. Garnish with lemon slices. Makes 35 to 40 appetizer servings.

Stuffed Snow Peas

These little green canoes will be the talk of the party.

1/2 lb. Chinese pea pods
1 (2-1/2-oz.) pkg. thinly sliced
  spiced beef
1 teaspoon prepared horseradish

1 cup dairy sour cream
1/2 teaspoon prepared mustard
1/8 teaspoon pepper

Trim ends from pea pods. In a medium saucepan, bring 3 cups lightly salted water to a boil. Carefully lower trimmed pea pods into boiling water. Simmer over medium heat about 1 minute until crisp-tender; drain. Immediately immerse pods in cold water. Drain again and refrigerate at least 30 minutes until chilled. Chop sliced beef very fine. In a small bowl, combine chopped beef, horseradish, sour cream, mustard and pepper. With a sharp knife, carefully slit 1 side of pea pod. Use a demitasse spoon or other small spoon to fill each pod with beef mixture. Arrange filled pods on baking sheet with raised sides, with pea pods touching to keep them upright. Refrigerate 1 hour; serve cold. Makes about 60 appetizer servings.

Jalapeño Pepper Jelly   Photo on pages 2 and 3.

Do not substitute pectin powder for the liquid pectin in this hot pepper jelly.

6 fresh jalapeño peppers, seeded,
  chopped
1 green bell pepper, seeded, chopped
1 cup vinegar

4 cups sugar
1 (3-oz.) pkg. or bottle liquid pectin
6 to 8 drops green food coloring,
  if desired

Sterilize four 7- or 8-ounce jelly jars with screw lids; keep hot. Line a large strainer or colander with 2 layers of cheesecloth; set aside. In blender or food processor, process jalapeño pepper, bell pepper and vinegar until pureed. In a 6- or 8-quart saucepan, combine pureed pepper mixture and sugar. Stirring constantly, bring to a full rolling boil over high heat. Quickly stir in pectin. Continue stirring while bringing to a full rolling boil that cannot be stirred down. Continue to stir and boil hard 1 minute. Remove from heat; use a metal spoon to skim foam from surface. Stir in green food coloring, if desired. Strain hot jelly through cheesecloth-lined strainer or colander, pressing mixture with back of spoon to strain all pulp possible. Discard pulp remaining in cheesecloth. Pour liquid into sterile jars; seal. Makes about 4 cups.

Variation
Substitute 2 fresh California green chili peppers for jalapeño peppers.

How to Make Stuffed Snow Peas

1/With a sharp knife cut open one side of blanched, chilled pea pods.

2/Fill split pea pods with meat mixture. Arrange on tray with sides touching; chill.

Salmon-Stuffed Tomatoes

Decorate your appetizer tray with these colorful bite-size morsels.

25 to 30 cherry tomatoes
1 (3-oz.) pkg. thinly sliced
  smoked salmon
1 (3-oz.) pkg. cream cheese,
  room temperature

1 teaspoon lemon juice
1 tablespoon minced watercress leaves
Salt and pepper to taste
Watercress sprigs for garnish

Cut a thin slice from stem-end of each tomato; scoop pulp and seeds from center with a small, sharp-edged spoon. Or make a deep X-cut from top of tomato almost to bottom; carefully pull tomato open at top and scoop out pulp and seeds. Turn tomatoes cut-side down on paper towels to drain. Chop salmon very fine. In a medium bowl, stir cream cheese until smooth. Stir in chopped salmon, lemon juice and 1 tablespoon minced watercress. Sprinkle inside of drained cherry tomatoes with salt and pepper to taste. Fill each with salmon mixture; top each with a small sprig of watercress. Makes 25 to 30 appetizer servings.

Stuffed Radish Roses

Quite a conversation starter!

2 bunches radishes (20 to 25)
1 (3-oz.) pkg. cream cheese,
  room temperature
2 tablespoons blue cheese, crumbled

1/8 teaspoon salt
1 tablespoon milk
1 tablespoon minced parsley

Cut stems and roots from radishes. Make deep X-cuts from top of radishes almost to bottoms. Let radishes stand in ice water 2 to 3 hours to open. In a small bowl, combine cream cheese, blue cheese, salt, milk and parsley. Drain radishes; pat dry with paper towels. Spoon cheese mixture into center and on top of each radish. Makes 20 to 25 appetizer servings.

Stuffed Ripe Olives

Serve these alone or to garnish a tray of assorted appetizers.

15 to 20 slender green onions
1 (6-oz. drained weight) can pitted
  extra large ripe olives
1/3 cup vegetable oil
2 tablespoons lemon juice

1/2 teaspoon dry mustard
1/4 teaspoon salt
1 tablespoon minced parsley
1 garlic clove, crushed
2 tablespoons grated Parmesan cheese

Cut each onion into 2 or 3 pieces about 1-1/2 inches long. With a sharp knife, make several 1/2-inch lengthwise cuts through 1 end of each piece of onion. Insert uncut end of onion into pitted olive. Cut end will open like a fan. Place onion-stuffed olives in an 8-inch, round cake pan; set aside. In a small bowl, combine remaining ingredients; pour over olives. Cover and refrigerate 6 hours or overnight. Drain before serving. Makes 40 to 45 appetizer servings.

Zucchini Bites

For better color and nutrition, shred the zucchini with the peel on.

2 eggs
2 medium zucchini, shredded
1 tablespoon dried minced onion
1 tablespoon chopped parsley
1/2 teaspoon salt

1/8 teaspoon pepper
1/4 cup fine dry breadcrumbs
2 tablespoons butter or margarine, melted
1 cup grated Cheddar cheese (4 oz.)

Grease an 8-inch square pan; set aside. Preheat oven to 350°F (175°C). In a medium bowl, beat eggs; stir in zucchini, onion, parsley, salt, pepper, breadcrumbs, butter or margarine and 1/2 cup Cheddar cheese. Spoon evenly into prepared pan; sprinkle with remaining cheese. Bake 20 to 25 minutes in preheated oven until set. Use a sharp knife to cut 7 rows vertically and 7 rows horizontally making 3/4-inch squares; serve warm. Makes 49 appetizer servings.

Stuffed Zucchini

Zucchini is easier to stuff when it is slightly undercooked.

4 small zucchini
1/4 cup butter or margarine, melted
1/2 cup grated Swiss cheese (2 oz.)
1/2 cup soft breadcrumbs
1/4 teaspoon salt

1/8 teaspoon pepper
1/8 teaspoon dried marjoram leaves,
 crumbled
2 tablespoons grated Parmesan cheese

In a medium saucepan with a tight-fitting lid, pour water to cover whole zucchini. Cook over medium heat until barely tender, 10 to 12 minutes. Cut in half lengthwise. Use a spoon to scoop out pulp, leaving a 1/4-inch shell. Do not puncture outer shell; set aside. Chop zucchini pulp very fine. Preheat oven to 375°F (190°C). In a medium bowl, combine pulp with butter or margarine, Swiss cheese, breadcrumbs, salt, pepper and marjoram. Spoon mixture evenly into zucchini shells. Sprinkle evenly with Parmesan cheese. Arrange in a 13'' x 9'' baking pan; bake 10 to 15 minutes in preheated oven until hot. Cut each stuffed zucchini half into 4 to 6 diagonal slices. Serve warm. Makes 32 to 48 appetizer servings.

Zucchini Pâté

This pâté is quite soft but excellent for spreading on crackers.

1/4 cup butter
4 zucchini, sliced
1 small onion, sliced
1/4 lb. mushrooms, chopped
1/2 teaspoon dried basil leaves
1/2 teaspoon salt

1/2 teaspoon curry powder
1 tablespoon lemon juice
1 hard-cooked egg, chopped
2 tablespoons mayonnaise
2 tablespoons grated Parmesan cheese

In a large skillet, melt butter. Add zucchini and onion; sauté 2 to 3 minutes until vegetables are soft. Stir in mushrooms, basil, salt and curry powder. Simmer 5 minutes. Stir in lemon juice, hard-cooked egg, mayonnaise and Parmesan cheese. In blender or food processor, puree mixture. Line a 1-quart plain mold or bowl with plastic wrap. Spoon zucchini mixture evenly into plastic-lined mold or bowl. Chill 6 hours or overnight. Invert onto a small platter or tray. Remove mold or bowl and plastic wrap. Mixture will be soft but will have general contour of container. Serve cold or reheat and serve warm. Makes about 3 cups.

Zucchini Appetizer Pie

Serve this soft, creamy pie on cocktail plates.

4 medium zucchini
2 tablespoons vegetable oil
2 eggs
1 cup cottage cheese
1/4 cup butter or margarine,
   room temperature
1/4 cup all-purpose flour

1/2 teaspoon baking powder
1/4 teaspoon salt
1 cup dairy sour cream
1/4 cup grated Parmesan cheese (1 oz.)
1 tomato, peeled, thinly sliced
Parsley sprigs for garnish

Cut zucchini crosswise into 1/4-inch slices. Heat oil in a large skillet. Add zucchini; sauté until softened but not mushy. Line bottom and side of a 9-inch pie plate with sautéed zucchini slices; set aside. Preheat oven to 350°F (175°C). In a large bowl, beat eggs. Beat in cottage cheese and butter or margarine until almost smooth. Stir in flour, baking powder and salt until blended. Stir in sour cream and Parmesan cheese until distributed. Pour evenly into zucchini-lined pic plate. Gently smooth top with spatula. Filling will not quite fill pan, but will expand when baked. Carefully arrange tomato slices over top of filling. Bake 35 to 45 minutes in preheated oven until firm in center. Cool on a rack 10 minutes. Invert onto a 12-inch round platter. Garnish center with parsley sprigs. Cut into small wedges; serve warm. Makes 16 to 20 appetizer servings.

How to Make Zucchini Appetizer Pie

1/Arrange sautéed zucchini slices over bottom and side of a 9-inch pie plate.

2/Pour in cheese filling without disturbing zucchini slices. Smooth surface with a spatula.

Zucchini Frittatas

Little morsels of chopped vegetables are held together with a puffy omelet-like mixture.

1/4 cup butter or margarine
4 green onions, thinly sliced
1/4 lb. mushrooms, chopped
2 medium zucchini, chopped
4 eggs
1 garlic clove, crushed

2 tablespoons minced parsley
1/2 teaspoon salt
1/8 teaspoon pepper
2 tablespoons butter or margarine
1/4 cup grated Parmesan cheese (1 oz.)

In a large skillet, melt 1/4 cup butter or margarine. Add onions, mushrooms and zucchini; sauté until vegetables are tender, about 2 minutes. Preheat oven to 400°F (205°C). In a medium bowl, beat eggs. Stir in garlic, parsley, salt, pepper and sautéed vegetables. Brush 2 tablespoons butter on bottom and sides of twenty-four 1-3/4-inch muffin cups. Heat cups in oven until butter or margarine sizzles. Spoon about 1 heaping tablespoon zucchini mixture into each muffin cup. Sprinkle tops evenly with Parmesan cheese. Bake 6 to 8 minutes in preheated oven until puffed and lightly browned. Cool on a rack 1 minute. Turn out of muffin cups; serve warm. Makes 24 appetizer servings.

3/Arrange thin peeled tomato slices closely together over top of filling; bake.

4/Cool baked pie 10 minutes. Invert onto platter and cut in wedges. Serve warm.

Pastries, Puffs & Things

Appetizers should be small enough to be finger foods. Bake pastries in small pans. Cut larger baked foods, such as Party Quiche, into small squares, thin strips or wedges so they can be easily picked up.

Pastries, puffs, breads, filo pastry, crepes and tortillas all form bases for delectable appetizers. They are especially convenient for the busy host or hostess because they can be made days ahead. Appetizer Pastry and Cream Cheese Pastry are rich and flaky. Use them or your favorite pastry recipe. When you are in a hurry, packaged pie-crust mixes are time and energy savers. You'll also find an appealing variety of fillings in this section. Experiment with different bases and fillings and listen to the compliments!

From the dough for one 9-inch double-crust pie you can make 40 to 45 miniature tart shells. Use 2-inch, scalloped tart pans to make small tarts that can be held comfortably in your fingers. These 3/4-inch-deep pans are also available in several other shapes—boats, triangles, squares and diamonds. Or use small muffin cups which also come in this size.

Appetizer Puffs and Petite Toast Cups are two additional finger-held appetizer containers. Appetizer Puffs are miniature puff pastry just the right size for an open house or reception refreshment. They are tasty when stuffed with Creamed Antipasto Filling or Curried Chicken Filling. You can also use Ham Filling, page 138, and Chicken or Turkey Filling, page 140.

Sandwiches made from refrigerator biscuits, such as Quick Pizzas and Herb Spirals, are deliciously different. Another innovative sandwich to spur conversation is Danish Crepewich, made from All-Purpose Crepes and filled with a mixture of eggs, anchovies, herbs and butter.

Appetizer Pastry

Freeze the extra baked shells to use at a later time.

1 cup butter, chilled
3-1/2 cups all-purpose flour
1/4 teaspoon salt

1 egg, slightly beaten
1/4 cup vegetable oil
1/2 cup cold water

Cut chilled butter into 1/2-inch slices. In a medium bowl, combine flour and salt. Use a pastry blender to cut in butter slices until mixture resembles oatmeal; set aside. In a small bowl, combine egg, oil and water. Using a fork, stir egg mixture into flour mixture until evenly distributed. Divide dough in half; shape into 2 balls. Wrap in plastic wrap or foil. Refrigerate at least 1 hour. Preheat oven to 400°F (205°C). **To make 9-inch pie shells,** roll out 1 ball of dough at a time on a lightly floured surface to a 10-inch circle. Fit into a 9-inch pie plate without stretching dough. Trim 1/2-inch larger than pie plate. Flute edge; prick bottom and side with tines of a fork. Repeat with remaining dough. **To make tart shells,** roll out dough as directed above. Use a 3-inch pastry cutter, top of a jar, bowl or drinking glass to cut dough into 3-inch circles. Carefully fit into 2-inch tart pans or muffin cups without stretching dough. Trim edges even with top of pans or cups; prick side and bottom of each with tines of a fork. Bake 10 to 12 minutes in preheated oven until golden brown; or fill with your favorite filling and bake according to that recipe's directions. Makes two 8- or 9-inch pastry shells or about 40 tart shells.

How to Make Tart Shells

1/Roll out pastry about 1/16 inch thick. Use a pastry cutter or drinking glass to cut pastry into 3-inch circles.

2/Without stretching dough, press pastry circle into tart pans with thumb or forefinger. Trim top even with tart pan.

Cream Cheese Tart Shells

Freeze the baked tart shells. Thaw and fill them just before serving.

**1/4 cup butter or margarine,
  room temperature**
**1 (3-oz.) pkg. cream cheese,
  room temperature**

3/4 cup all-purpose flour

In a medium bowl, stir butter or margarine and cream cheese until smooth. Use a pastry blender or fork to cut in flour until particles resemble small peas. Shape into a ball. Wrap in plastic wrap or foil; refrigerate 4 or 6 hours or overnight. Preheat oven to 425°F (220°C). On a lightly floured surface, roll out dough to a 15" x 9" rectangle. Cut dough into fifteen 3-inch circles or squares. Press into 2- to 2-1/2-inch tart pans or muffin cups. Trim and flute edges. Prick with a fork. Bake 10 to 15 minutes in preheated oven until golden brown. Makes 15 tart shells.

Miniature Cheese Shells

Fill the shells with a meat filling just before serving.

1/2 cup butter, room temperature
**1 (3-oz.) pkg. cream cheese,
  room temperature**

1/4 teaspoon salt
1/4 cup grated Parmesan cheese (1 oz.)
1 cup all-purpose flour

In a medium bowl, combine butter and cream cheese until smooth. Stir in salt, Parmesan cheese and flour until blended. Shape into a ball; wrap in waxed paper or foil. Refrigerate 1 hour. Preheat oven to 425°F (220°C). Roll out dough on a lightly floured surface to about 1/8-inch thickness. Cut into 3-1/2-inch circles. Press over bottoms and up sides of 2-inch tart pans or muffin cups. Bake 5 to 7 minutes in preheated oven until golden brown. Makes 20 to 25 tart shells.

California Onion Cakes

You can also brown these sandwiches in a skillet or on a griddle.

1 (9/16-oz.) pkg. dry green onion dip mix
3/4 cup dairy sour cream
1 cup grated Cheddar cheese (4 oz.)

1/4 cup grated Parmesan cheese (1 oz.)
8 (7-inch) flour tortillas
2 to 3 tablespoons vegetable oil

In a small bowl, combine green onion dip mix, sour cream, Cheddar cheese and Parmesan cheese. Preheat broiler if necessary. Place oven rack 5 to 8 inches from heating element. Arrange 2 tortillas in a single layer on each of 2 ungreased baking sheets. Spread cheese mixture evenly over tortillas; top with remaining tortillas. Brush tops evenly with oil. Broil tortilla stacks until puffy and lightly browned. Turn bottom sides up and brush with oil. Repeat broiling. Cut each sandwich into 8 wedges; serve warm. Makes 32 appetizer servings.

Appetizer Puffs   Photo on page 95.

Fill these puffs with meat, vegetable, fruit or cheese fillings.

1/4 cup butter or margarine	**1/8 teaspoon salt**
1/2 cup water	**2 eggs**
1/2 cup all-purpose flour	

Lightly grease 2 large baking sheets; set aside. Preheat oven to 400°F (205°C). In a medium saucepan, heat butter or margarine and water to a rolling boil. Add flour and salt all at once. Stir vigorously over low heat about 1 minute or until mixture becomes smooth and leaves side of pan. Remove from heat. Beat in eggs, one at a time. Beat until mixture looses its gloss. On pre-pared baking sheet, drop dough by mounded teaspoonfuls making 4 rows with 4 mounds in each row. Repeat with remaining dough on second baking sheet. Bake about 15 minutes in preheated oven until puffed and lightly browned. Cool away from draft. Makes 32 puffs.

Herbed Pull-Apart Cheese Puffs

Puffs run together while they're baking, but they pull apart easily.

1/2 cup water	**1 green onion, minced**
1/4 cup milk	**1/2 teaspoon dried basil leaves, crushed**
1/3 cup butter or margarine	**1 tablespoon minced parsley**
3/4 cup all-purpose flour	**1/2 teaspoon dried dill weed**
1/4 teaspoon salt	**1/2 teaspoon dry mustard**
3 eggs	**1 egg, slightly beaten**
1 cup grated Swiss cheese (4 oz.)	**1/4 teaspoon salt**

Grease a large baking sheet; set aside. Preheat oven to 400°F (205°C). In a medium saucepan, bring water, milk, and butter or margarine to a boil. Add flour and 1/4 teaspoon salt all at once. Stir vigorously over low heat about 1 minute or until mixture becomes smooth and leaves side of pan. Remove from heat. Beat in 3 eggs, one at a time. Beat with a spoon after each addition until mixture is shiny and smooth. Beat in cheese, onion, basil, parsley, dill weed and mustard. On prepared baking sheet, form a 12-inch circle by spooning heaping teaspoonfuls of dough in 17 or 18 small mounds about 1/2-inch apart. In a small bowl, combine 1 slightly beaten egg and 1/4 teaspoon salt. Brush egg mixture over top of each mound of dough. Bake 18 to 22 minutes in pre-heated oven until puffed and golden. Serve warm or cool. Makes 17 or 18 appetizer servings.

Thaw frozen appetizer shells or puffs in their freezer wrap at room temperature about 1 hour.

Petite Toast Cups

Process the crusts in your blender to make breadcrumbs to use in other recipes.

6 slices sandwich bread

Preheat oven to 350°F (175°C). Remove crusts from bread; cut each slice into 4 equal squares. Carefully press each square into a 2-inch muffin cup or miniature tart pan. Bake 10 to 15 minutes in preheated oven until lightly browned. Remove from oven. Cool and freeze or fill with desired filling. Makes 24 toast cups.

Tangy Cheese Cups

Serve these piquant appetizers with hot and cold beverages.

8 slices sandwich bread
1/4 cup butter or margarine,
  room temperature
1 cup grated Swiss cheese (4 oz.)
1 tablespoon minced parsley

1 teaspoon prepared horseradish
1 teaspoon prepared mustard
1/4 teaspoon salt
1 egg white
Paprika for garnish

Remove crusts from bread; cut each slice into 4 equal squares. Gently press each bread square into a 2-inch muffin cup or tart pan; set aside. Preheat oven to 400°F (205°C). In a small bowl, combine butter or margarine, cheese, parsley, horseradish, mustard and salt. Stir in egg white. Spoon about 1 teaspoon cheese mixture into each bread-lined muffin cup or tart pan. Sprinkle with paprika for garnish. Bake 5 to 8 minutes in preheated oven until bread is golden brown and cheese is melted. Remove baked cups from pans; serve hot. Makes 32 appetizer servings.

How to Make Petite Toast Cups

1/Trim crusts from bread. Cut each trimmed slice into four squares.

2/With index finger or thumb, lightly press squares into miniature muffin cups.

Deviled Egg & Pepperoni Cups

Make the toast cups ahead and fill them just before serving time.

3 hard-cooked eggs, finely chopped
3 tablespoons mayonnaise
2 tablespoons minced green onion
2 teaspoons minced parsley
1 teaspoon prepared mustard
1/4 teaspoon Worcestershire sauce

1/8 teaspoon salt
10 thin slices pepperoni, finely chopped
24 Petite Toast Cups, page 78
1/3 cup finely grated Swiss cheese
  (about 1-1/2 oz.)

In a medium bowl, combine eggs, mayonnaise, onion, parsley, mustard, Worcestershire sauce, salt and pepperoni. Preheat oven to 350°F (175°C). Spoon egg mixture evenly into toast cups. Arrange filled toast cups on an ungreased baking sheet. Sprinkle cheese evenly over filling. Bake 10 to 15 minutes in preheated oven until cheese melts. Serve warm. Makes 24 appetizer servings.

Golden Fish Triangles

If smoked fish is not available, substitute anchovy fillets.

8 thin slices firm white bread
4 thin slices mozzarella cheese
  (about 4 oz.)
3 or 4 oz. smoked albacore or
  swordfish, thinly sliced

2 tablespoons butter
3 eggs, beaten slightly
2 teaspoon minced fresh chives
2 small tomatoes, thinly sliced then halved

Preheat oven to 400F (205C). Trim and discard bread crusts. Cover 4 slices bread with mozzarella cheese. Top with slices of smoked fish; then cover each with remaining bread slices. Melt butter in 13'' x 9'' pan in oven. Spread butter out in pan. In shallow dish combine eggs and chives. Dip each sandwich in egg mixture; coating all sides. Place in prepared pan. Repeat until all sandwiches are coated. Bake in preheated oven 12 to 14 minutes or until bread turns a light golden color. Cut each sandwich into four triangles. Stand 8 triangles on one of their narrow sides, in a circle, on a serving plate. Fill center of circle with overlapping half slices of one tomato. On second serving plate, form circle with remaining triangles and fill center with tomato slices. Makes 16 triangles.

Royal Seafood Tarts

Pastry for a single 9-inch crust will make twenty 2-inch pastry shells.

1 tablespoon butter or margarine
1/4 cup chopped mushrooms
1 tablespoon tomato paste
1 tablespoon lemon juice
1 teaspoon Worcestershire sauce
1/2 cup dairy sour cream

1/2 teaspoon prepared horseradish
1 cup chopped cooked shrimp or crab
20 baked Appetizer Pastry Tart Shells,
  page 75
1/2 cup grated Swiss cheese (2 oz.)

In a medium skillet, melt butter or margarine. Add mushrooms; sauté about 3 minutes. Stir in tomato paste, lemon juice, Worcestershire sauce, sour cream, horseradish and shrimp or crab. Stir occasionally over low heat until heated through; do not boil. Preheat oven to 400°F (205°C). Spoon seafood mixture evenly into baked tart shells. Sprinkle evenly with Swiss cheese. Bake 10 to 15 minutes in preheated oven until cheese is bubbly. Arrange on a tray or serving plate; serve warm. Makes 20 appetizer servings.

Avocado & Crab Filling

Smash your piggy bank and splurge! This is an outstanding filling.

6 oz. cooked fresh crab or
   1 (6-oz.) pkg. frozen crabmeat
1 avocado, mashed
1 tablespoon lemon juice
2 tablespoons minced chives

2 tablespoons plain yogurt
1/8 teaspoon chili powder
1/4 teaspoon salt
18 to 20 Miniature Cheese Shells,
   page 76

If using frozen crabmeat, thaw and drain. In a medium bowl, use 2 forks to flake crabmeat. Stir in mashed avocado, lemon juice, chives, yogurt, chili powder and salt. Spoon about 1 tablespoon crabmeat mixture into each tart shell. Makes 18 to 20 appetizer servings.

Creamed Antipasto Filling   Photo on page 95.

For the best results, fill the cream puffs or tart shells just before serving.

2 tablespoons butter or margarine
1/2 lb. mushrooms, finely chopped
1/4 cup minced green onions
1/8 teaspoon salt
1/4 cup dairy sour cream

1/2 cup minced salami or dried beef
28 to 30 Appetizer Puffs, page 77, or
   baked Appetizer Pastry Tart Shells,
   page 75

In a large skillet, melt butter or margarine. Add mushrooms and onions; sauté 1 to 2 minutes until tender. Stir in salt, sour cream and salami or beef. Spoon about 1 tablespoon filling into each cream puff or tart shell. Makes 28 to 30 appetizer servings.

Curried Chicken Filling

For special occasions, use this filling in Appetizer Puffs, page 77.

2 cups finely chopped, cooked chicken
1/4 cup finely chopped celery
1 small apple, peeled, cored,
   coarsely grated
1 tablespoon chopped chives
1/3 cup mayonnaise

2 teaspoons curry powder
1/4 teaspoon salt
1/4 cup finely chopped peanuts
24 Petite Toast Cups, page 78, or
   baked Appetizer Pastry Tart Shells,
   page 75

In a medium bowl, combine chicken, celery, apple, chives, mayonnaise, curry powder, salt and peanuts. Spoon about 1-1/2 tablespoons filling into each toast cup or tart shell. Makes 24 appetizer servings.

Bacon & Mushroom Roll-Ups

Frozen roll-ups take eighteen to twenty minutes to bake.

4 slices lean bacon, diced
1/2 lb. mushrooms, chopped
1 medium onion, chopped
1/2 teaspoon salt
1/8 teaspoon pepper

1 (3-oz.) pkg. cream cheese,
  room temperature
12 slices sandwich bread
1/4 cup butter, melted

In a large skillet, sauté bacon, mushrooms, onion, salt and pepper 5 to 8 minutes. Bacon will not be crisp. Stir in cream cheese; set aside. Cut crusts from bread. With a rolling pin, flatten each trimmed slice of bread until 1/4-inch thick. Spread about 2 tablespoons mushroom mixture evenly over each flattened bread slice. With filling-side up, roll each slice jelly-roll fashion. Secure roll-ups with wooden picks if necessary. Refrigerate at least 1 hour or freeze, if desired. Remove from freezer about 40 minutes before baking. Preheat oven to 375°F (190°C). Arrange roll-ups on an ungreased baking sheet; brush each with melted butter. Bake 10 to 15 minutes until lightly browned. Leave baked roll-ups whole or cut each in half. Serve warm. Makes 12 whole roll-ups or 24 appetizer servings.

Brie en Croûte

Pastry dough is easier to roll when it has been chilled at least one hour.

1 (3-oz.) pkg. cream cheese,
  room temperature
1/4 cup butter, room temperature

3/4 cup all-purpose flour
1 (4-1/2-oz.) pkg. Brie cheese
1/2 teaspoon sesame seeds

In a medium bowl, cut cream cheese and butter into flour with a pastry blender until particles resemble small peas. Shape into a ball. Wrap in foil or plastic wrap; refrigerate at least 1 hour. Divide dough into 2 pieces. On a lightly floured surface, roll out each piece about 1/8-inch thick. Cut each into a 6-inch circle, reserving excess dough for trim. Place 1 circle of dough on an ungreased baking sheet. Place whole Brie cheese in center of dough; top with other pastry circle. Pinch pastry edges together to seal. Preheat oven to 400°F (205°C). Roll out excess dough. Cut 1 decorative design with a cookie cutter and about 10 small designs with hors d'oeuvre cutters. Place large cut-out on top of croûte and small cut-outs around side. Sprinkle with sesame seeds. Bake 15 to 17 minutes in preheated oven until golden brown. Let stand several minutes before cutting into small wedges. Serve warm. Makes 16 to 18 appetizer servings.

Spinach-Cheese Pie

Spinach and dill flavors are nicely blended in a rich sauce with feta cheese.

1 (10-oz.) pkg. frozen chopped spinach
Appetizer Pastry dough, page 75 or
  pie dough of choice
2 tablespoons vegetable oil
1 large onion, chopped
3 eggs
1/4 lb. feta cheese, crumbled
  (about 1 cup)
1 teaspoon dried dill weed
1/2 teaspoon salt
1/8 teaspoon pepper

Place spinach in a strainer or colander to thaw and drain. Divide pastry dough into 2 pieces. Roll out 1 piece to a 12-inch circle. Gently fit over bottom and up side of a 9-inch pie pan or quiche pan. Roll out remaining pastry to a 10-inch circle; set aside. Pour oil into a large skillet; add onion. Sauté over medium heat 2 to 3 minutes until softened. With back of a large spoon, press excess water out of thawed spinach. Stir drained spinach into sautéed onion. Stir occasionally over medium heat 4 to 5 minutes until spinach is limp; set aside. Preheat oven to 350°F (175°C). In a medium bowl, beat eggs. Stir in cheese, dill, salt, pepper and spinach mixture. Spoon into pastry-lined pan. Top with remaining pastry. Trim and crimp edges. Cut several slits in top pastry. Bake 50 to 60 minutes until golden brown. Cool about 10 minutes before serving. Cut into small wedges. Makes 16 to 20 appetizer servings.

How to Make Brie en Croûte

1/Roll pastry 1/8 inch thick; cut two 6-inch circles. Lay cheese on one circle; cover with remaining circle.

2/Flute edges to seal. Cut decorative shapes from remaining dough; use to decorate croûte.

Open-Face Tacos

Cans of round tortilla chips are displayed with potato chips in most supermarkets.

1 lb. lean ground beef
1 (1-1/4-oz.) pkg. taco seasoning mix
1 cup water
1 (5-1/2-oz.) can round flat
  2-1/2-inch tortilla chips

2 cups grated Cheddar cheese (8 oz.)
2 medium tomatoes, chopped
1 avocado, thinly sliced
1/2 cup dairy sour cream, if desired

In a medium skillet, cook beef until browned, stirring with a fork or spoon to crumble meat. Drain and discard drippings. Stir in taco seasoning mix and water. Bring to a boil. Simmer 10 to 15 minutes, stirring occasionally. Arrange a single layer of tortilla chips on an ungreased baking sheet. Preheat broiler if necessary. Place oven rack 5 to 8 inches from heating element. Spoon about 2 teaspoons meat mixture on each chip. Sprinkle cheese evenly over chips. Place under broiler until bubbly. Top each chip with about 2 pieces tomato and 1 avocado slice. Top with sour cream, if desired. Serve immediately. Makes 45 to 50 appetizer servings.

Won Tons

Buy frozen or refrigerated wrappers in gourmet shops or in your supermarket.

1/2 lb. ground pork
4 large uncooked shrimp, shelled,
  deveined
4 water chestnuts, finely chopped
1 green onion, finely chopped
1 egg, slightly beaten

1 tablespoon soy sauce
1/2 teaspoon salt
1/8 teaspoon pepper
50 won ton wrappers
Oil for deep-frying

In a small skillet, sauté pork until browned. Remove and discard drippings. Chop shrimp very fine. Stir shrimp, water chestnuts and onion into sautéed pork. Cook and stir about 2 minutes. Stir in egg, soy sauce, salt and pepper. Spoon about 1-1/2 teaspoons pork mixture on center of each won ton wrapper. Moisten edges of wrappers with water. Fold two opposite corners together over filling, making a triangle. Press edges together to seal. Pour oil for deep-frying into a deep-fryer to depth recommended by manufacturer or pour oil 2 inches deep in a heavy medium saucepan. Heat oil to 375°F (190°C). At this temperature a 1-inch cube of bread will turn golden brown in 40 seconds. Lower won tons into hot oil one at a time. Fry about 1 minute until crisp and golden brown. Drain on paper towels; serve hot. Makes about 50 appetizer servings.

Beef Turnovers

Cut the dough circles larger and fill with more meat mixture, but expect fewer turnovers.

1/2 lb. lean ground beef
2 tablespoons chopped onion
2 tablespoons chopped green pepper
1 small tomato, seeded, diced
1/2 teaspoon salt
1/8 teaspoon pepper

1 tablespoon cornstarch
1/2 cup beef broth or bouillon
1 tablespoon finely chopped almonds
2 tablespoons chopped raisins
Appetizer Pastry dough, page 75 or
    pie dough of choice

In a medium skillet, sauté ground beef until browned. Drain and discard drippings. Stir in onion, green pepper, tomato, salt and pepper. Stir cornstarch into beef broth or bouillon until dissolved. Stir into meat mixture. Cook and stir about 4 minutes until mixture is slightly thickened. Remove from heat. Stir in almonds and raisins; cool slightly. Preheat oven to 400°F (205°C). On a lightly floured surface, roll out pastry to a 22" x 15" rectangle. Cut into 3-inch circles. Spoon 1 to 2 tablespoons filling on center of each circle. Fold dough over filling; press edges with tines of a fork to seal. Puncture top with tines of fork to let steam escape. Repeat with excess dough. Arrange on 2 ungreased baking sheets. Bake 12 to 15 minutes in preheated oven until golden brown. Serve warm. Makes 35 to 38 appetizer servings.

All-Purpose Crepes

Freeze extra crepes in airtight freezer containers, bags or wrap.

4 eggs
1/4 teaspoon salt
2 cups all-purpose flour

2-1/4 cups milk
1/4 cup vegetable oil or butter, melted

In a medium bowl, beat eggs and salt with a whisk or an electric mixer. Gradually add flour alternately with milk, beating until smooth. Beat in oil or butter. If batter contains bubbles, refrigerate for about 1 hour until most bubbles disappear. Stir refrigerated batter before cooking. Preheat traditional crepe pan or upside-down crepe pan. In traditional crepe pan, spoon 2 to 3 tablespoons batter onto surface, quickly tipping pan from side to side until batter covers bottom of pan. Cook until bottom is browned, 1 to 1-1/2 minutes, then turn with a spatula and bake other side 5 to 7 seconds. If using an upside-down crepe pan, dip rounded top of preheated pan into batter. Cook until crepe is lightly browned around edge. It is not necessary to cook other side. Place cooked crepe in a covered deep dish or pan. Use immediately or stack with waxed paper between crepes. Wrap stacked crepes in freezer wrap or freeze in a plastic bag or container. Store in freezer; use within 6 months. Makes 30 to 35 crepes.

How to Make Beef Turnovers

1/Spoon 1 to 2 tablespoons meat mixture onto center of each 3-inch pastry circle.

2/Fold top half of pastry over filling. Crimp edges with a fork to seal.

Danish Crepewich

The flavors are Danish but the shape is French.

1 (2-oz.) can flat anchovy fillets,
  drained
1/4 cup butter or margarine,
  room temperature
2 tablespoons Dijon-style mustard
4 hard-cooked eggs, finely chopped
1/4 teaspoon dried dill weed
2 teaspoons finely chopped parsley
2 teaspoons finely chopped chives

1/4 teaspoon pepper
1/2 small cucumber, finely chopped
6 (6-inch) cooked All-Purpose Crepes,
  opposite page
2 tablespoons minced parsley for garnish
3 thin slices cucumber, quartered,
  for garnish
3 cherry tomatoes, halved, for garnish

Finely chop anchovies. In a medium bowl, combine chopped anchovies, butter or margarine, mustard, eggs, dill weed, 2 teaspoons parsley, chives, pepper and chopped cucumber. Spread evenly on cooked crepes. Layer coated crepes to make a 6-layer stack. Spoon 2 tablespoons chopped parsley for garnish in a ring around edge of top crepe. Complete garnishing with cucumber pieces and cherry tomato halves. To serve, cut into wedges. Makes one 6-inch stack or about 12 appetizer servings.

Greek Roll-Ups

Look for frozen filo in your supermarket or in Greek specialty food stores.

1 cup grated sharp Cheddar cheese (4 oz.)
1/4 cup finely chopped ripe olives
1 tablespoon minced green onion

6 sheets filo dough
1/2 cup butter, melted

In a small bowl, combine cheese, olives and onion; set aside. Lightly grease a large baking sheet; set aside. Preheat oven to 375°F (190°C). Place 1 sheet filo dough on a flat surface. Cover remaining filo sheets with a damp towel to prevent drying. Brush filo sheet with melted butter. Top with 2 more filo sheets, brushing each with butter. Spoon half of the cheese mixture across 1 long end of layered dough. Beginning with side containing cheese mixture, carefully roll up jelly-roll fashion, making a tight roll. Place seam-side down on prepared baking sheet. Brush top with butter. Repeat with remaining filo sheets and filling. Bake 10 to 15 minutes in preheated oven until bubbly and golden brown. Cut each roll into 1-1/2- to 2-inch lengths. Serve warm. Makes 16 to 20 appetizer servings.

Trojan Triangles

The fold used here is similar to the way a flag is folded.

4 oz. feta cheese, crumbled (about 1 cup)
1/2 cup cottage cheese
1 egg, slightly beaten

1 tablespoon minced parsley
4 sheets filo dough
1/4 cup butter, melted

Lightly butter a large baking sheet; set aside. In a small bowl, mix feta cheese and cottage cheese; stir in egg and parsley; set aside. Brush 1 sheet filo dough with melted butter. Cut buttered sheet into strips about 2 inches wide. Cover all filo dough with a damp towels to prevent drying. Remove 1 strip from beneath towels. With short end of strip on side closest to you, spoon about 1 level tablespoon cheese mixture on left-hand corner of strip. Fold corner with filling up and to the right, making a diagonal fold. Now lift lower point of dough. Fold straight up and away from you, keeping right-hand edges of dough together. Fold right-hand corner of dough up and to the left, again making a diagonal fold. Lift lower point of dough and fold straight up and away from you. Continue folding filled filo dough until all of dough strip is folded into a multiple-layered triangle. Brush top with melted butter. Repeat with remaining filo dough and filling. Arrange folded filo dough on baking sheet. Preheat oven to 375°F (190°C). Bake 10 to 15 minutes until puffy and golden brown. Serve warm. Makes 24 to 30 appetizer servings.

If you freeze and later thaw miniature cream puff shells, heat them in the oven a few minutes to crisp the outside before filling them.

Quick Pizzas

Teenagers are delighted with these small pizzas.

1 (12-oz.) pkg. refrigerated large
  buttermilk biscuits
1 (8-oz.) can tomato sauce
1 garlic clove, crushed
1/4 teaspoon dried thyme leaves, crushed
1/4 teaspoon dried oregano leaves,
  crushed

1/8 teaspoon pepper
40 slices pepperoni (3-1/2 to 4 oz.)
1/2 cup chopped mushrooms
1/2 cup grated mozzarella cheese (2 oz.)

Preheat oven to 425°F (220°C). Separate biscuits; cut each into 4 equal pieces. Roll each piece into a ball between palms of your hands. On an ungreased baking sheet, use the heel of your hand to flatten each ball into a 2-inch circle. Pinch edges to make a shallow rim; set aside. In a small bowl, combine tomato sauce, garlic, thyme, oregano and pepper. Spread about 1-1/2 teaspoons sauce evenly over each flattened biscuit. Top each with 1 pepperoni slice, about 1/2 teaspoon mushrooms and about 1/2 teaspoon cheese. Bake about 10 minutes in preheated oven until biscuits are golden brown. Serve warm. Makes 40 appetizer servings.

Herb Spirals

These are not only super-tasting, but inexpensive and simple to prepare.

2 tablespoons butter or margarine
3 green onions, finely chopped
1 garlic clove, crushed
1/2 cup minced parsley
1 teaspoon dried oregano leaves, crushed

1/2 teaspoon salt
1 (8-oz.) pkg. refrigerated crescent rolls
1/3 cup grated Parmesan cheese
  (about 1-1/2 oz.)

In a small saucepan, melt butter or margarine. Add onions, garlic, parsley, oregano and salt. Sauté 2 to 3 minutes until onions are tender; set aside. Preheat oven to 375°F (190°C). Remove crescent rolls from package without separating at perforations. With 4 of dough pieces still joined, press with your fingers to seal at perforations, making a square. Roll out dough to a 9-inch square. Sprinkle with half of the onion mixture and half of the cheese. Roll up jelly-roll fashion. Use a sharp knife to cut into 1/2-inch slices. Repeat with remaining ingredients. Bake about 8 minutes in preheated oven until golden brown. Makes 32 to 36 appetizer servings.

Bacon & Mushroom Quiches

Don't prick the pastry or the filling will seep into it and become soggy.

4 slices lean bacon, finely chopped
1/4 lb. mushrooms, chopped
1/4 cup chopped green onions
1/4 teaspoon salt

40 unbaked Appetizer Pastry tart shells,
   page 75
3 eggs
1 cup dairy sour cream

In a medium skillet, fry bacon until most of fat is removed; drain drippings from skillet. Add mushrooms, onions and salt. Stirring occasionally, cook over medium heat until vegetables are tender, about 3 minutes. Set aside to cool. Preheat oven to 375°F (190°C). Divide bacon mixture evenly among unbaked tart shells; set aside. Beat eggs; stir in sour cream. Spoon evenly over bacon mixture. Bake 20 to 25 minutes in preheated oven. Serve warm. Makes about 40 appetizer servings.

Party Quiche

If these are made into tart shells, bake them 20 to 25 minutes at 375°F (190°C).

4 slices lean bacon, chopped
1 onion, chopped
2 tablespoons all-purpose flour
4 eggs
1-1/2 cups milk
1/2 teaspoon salt

1/8 teaspoon pepper
1-1/2 cups grated Swiss cheese (6 oz.)
Appetizer Pastry dough, page 75 or
   pie dough of choice
1 egg white
1/4 cup grated Parmesan cheese (1 oz.)

In a medium skillet, sauté bacon and onion until most of fat is cooked out of bacon, 7 to 10 minutes. Remove from heat; drain. Stir flour into drained bacon mixture. In a large bowl, beat eggs; stir in milk, salt, pepper, Swiss cheese and bacon mixture. Preheat oven to 350°F (175°C). On a lightly floured surface, roll out pastry to a 17'' x 12'' rectangle. Fit onto an ungreased 15'' x 10'' baking sheet with raised sides. Turn under and crimp edge of pastry. Brush with unbeaten egg white. Spoon cheese filling evenly over coated pastry. Sprinkle evenly with Parmesan cheese. Bake 30 to 40 minutes in preheated oven until filling is partially set and surface is golden brown. Filling will continue to bake when removed from oven. To serve, cut into small squares; serve warm. Makes 50 to 60 appetizer servings.

Bake quiches in square or rectangular pans then cut in small squares or rectangles for easy-to-handle pieces.

Pâtés, Molds & Spreads

Pâtés, molds and *spreads* are the backbone of refreshments at formal or informal gatherings. Serve them singly or in combination for flavor, color and texture contrasts. Add several nibblers or dippers, some savory nuts and a drink for a complete menu. Some of these appetizers take several hours to complete. Others, such as Sampan Spread and Deviled Ham & Cheese, can be whipped up at a moment's notice for unexpected guests.

If you can make meat loaf, you will enjoy making pâtés. Just think of them as elegant meat loaves with a French accent. Most people visualize pâtés as smooth mixtures of pureed chicken livers, butter and seasonings. Many smooth and chunky pâtés contain no liver. In France, refrigerated cases in *Charcuteries*, or meat shops, are lined with a fascinating assortment of pâtés. They may contain cooked ground pork, fully-cooked ham, chopped pistachio nuts or chopped cooked duck. You'll find an equally delicious variety of pâtés in this section.

Terrine originally referred to a special decorative container for pâtés. Today, it also describes a pâté baked in a bacon-lined terrine or a 9" x 5" loaf pan which is placed in another pan of hot water. Traditionally, meats used in terrines are compacted by placing a heavy object on top of the meat while it cooks and as it cools. They are easier to slice after being pressed, but the process is not essential.

When serving a pâté or terrine on a tray, decorate for color and texture with cluster of fruit, carrot slices, radish roses, stuffed olives or watercress sprigs.

Molds bring interesting shapes to otherwise small or shapeless appetizers. Use crocks or bowls as molds, or add interest by molding mixtures in crown, fluted, star or fish molds. To unmold, gently run a small spatula between the mixture and the mold. Or dip the mold in and out of warm water two or three times, then invert onto a tray or platter. When you remove the mold, the mixture will be softly set, yet hold its shape. Fill the centers of ring molds with colorful garnishes such as parsley sprigs, carrot curls or cherry tomatoes. Your garnishes will also be eaten as appetizers.

Spreads are often considered the poor relative of more elegant pâtés or molds, but they are delightfully easy to prepare. These make-ahead treats will keep several hours or several days in the refrigerator. Add a fresh garnish of radish slices, slivers of green onion or pickle slices and they are ready to serve.

Marinated Pâté

You'll need to prepare this the day before serving so it will be thoroughly chilled.

1 whole uncooked chicken breast
2 uncooked chicken thighs
1/2 cup dry white wine
1/2 teaspoon salt
1/4 teaspoon pepper
1/2 teaspoon dried thyme leaves
2 whole cloves

12 oz. pork sausage
1 egg, slightly beaten
1 garlic clove, crushed
1/8 teaspoon ground allspice
6 slices bacon
French bread, sliced, or crackers

Remove skin and bones from chicken breast and thighs. Cut chicken meat into 1/2-inch cubes. In a medium bowl, combine chicken cubes, wine, salt, pepper, thyme and cloves. Marinate in refrigerator 6 hours or overnight. Drain; reserve marinade. Remove and discard whole cloves. In another medium bowl, combine 1/4 cup reserved marinade, sausage, egg, garlic and allspice; set aside. Preheat oven to 350°F (175°C). Line a 1-1/2-quart casserole dish with bacon, letting ends extend over side. Arrange drained marinated chicken over bacon. Spoon sausage mixture over chicken. Press with the back of a spoon to pack. Pour remaining marinade over sausage mixture. Fold bacon ends over top of pâté. Cover tightly with lid or foil. Bake 1-1/2 hours in preheated oven. Spoon off drippings. To pack pâté, top with a plate. Place a can or other heavy item on top of plate. Cool on a rack 30 minutes. Refrigerate 6 hours or overnight. Pour off drippings. Invert casserole onto a small platter; remove dish. Remove bacon if desired. Slice and serve with French bread or crackers. Makes about 1 quart or 35 to 40 appetizer servings.

How to Make Marinated Pâté

1/Line a round, oval, or rectangular casserole or terrine with bacon slices, letting ends extend over side of dish.

2/Spoon sausage mixture over chicken. Pack by pressing with back of a spoon.

Layered Pâté

It's not as complicated as it seems; follow the directions, one step at a time.

8 slices bacon
2 eggs
1/8 teaspoon ground allspice
1/4 teaspoon dried thyme leaves
1-1/2 teaspoons salt
1/4 teaspoon pepper
1/4 teaspoon dried marjoram leaves
1 garlic clove, crushed
3 shallots or green onions,
   finely chopped

1 lb. ground chicken or turkey
1/2 lb. ground pork
1/4 cup dry white wine
6 slices boiled or baked ham
1/4 cup whole, shelled,
   green pistachio nuts
French bread, sliced, or Melba toast

Line a 7" x 3" loaf pan or ovenproof terrine with bacon, letting bacon ends extend over side; set aside. Preheat oven to 350°F (175°C). In a large bowl, combine eggs, allspice, thyme, salt, pepper, marjoram, garlic and onions. Stir in ground chicken or turkey, ground pork and wine. Press about 1/2 of the meat mixture into bacon-lined pan. Arrange ham slices in 2 or 3 layers over meat mixture; scatter pistachio nuts evenly over ham. Carefully spoon remaining meat mixture over ham and nuts. Bring ends of bacon slices over meat mixture. Cover with foil. Place loaf pan or terrine containing pâté in an 11" x 7" baking pan. Pour about 1 inch boiling water into outer pan. Bake 1-3/4 hours in preheated oven. Place another 7" x 3" loaf pan on top of cooked pâté. Place a heavy object in top pan. Refrigerate weighted pâté at least 4 hours to thoroughly chill. To serve, cut into 12 to 15 slices; cut each slice in half. Serve with French bread or Melba toast. Makes one 7" x 3" loaf or 24 to 30 appetizer servings.

3/Pour remaining marinade over sausage mixture. Fold bacon ends over top of pâté.

4/Cover dish with lid or foil, crimping edge of foil to make a tight cover.

Velvety Chicken Liver Pâté

So smooth it melts in your mouth, yet quick to make.

1/4 cup butter
1/2 lb. chicken livers, halved
1 small onion, chopped
1 small tart apple, peeled, cored,
    chopped
1/2 teaspoon salt

1/8 teaspoon pepper
2 tablespoons brandy
2 tablespoons whipping cream
1/4 cup butter, room temperature
Crackers or Melba toast rounds

In a medium skillet, melt 1/4 cup butter. Add chicken livers; sauté 2 minutes. Add onion, apple, salt and pepper. Cook and stir over medium heat about 5 minutes until apple softens. Stir in brandy and cream. Spoon mixture into blender or food processor. Process 2 to 3 minutes or until smooth. Refrigerate about 1 hour or until completely cooled. In a medium bowl, beat 1/4 cup room temperature butter until fluffy; gradually beat in cooled liver mixture. Spoon into a small crock or bowl. Cover and refrigerate at least 2 hours before serving with crackers or Melba toast rounds. Makes 2 cups.

Poor Man's Pâté

Serve this reasonably priced pâté with decorative crackers or slices of French bread.

2 slices bacon, chopped
1 small onion, chopped
1 carrot, peeled, finely chopped
6 uncooked chicken thighs
1/2 lb. ground pork
1 tablespoon chopped parsley

1/4 teaspoon ground ginger
1/8 teaspoon poultry seasoning
1 teaspoon salt
1/4 teaspoon pepper
Pinch ground allspice

In a medium skillet, cook bacon, onion and carrot until carrots are crisp-tender, about 5 minutes; set aside. Remove and discard skin and bones from chicken thighs. Cut meat into 1/2-inch pieces. Sauté cut up chicken and ground pork in skillet with bacon mixture until meat is browned. Use a slotted spoon to place meat mixture in blender or food processor. Spoon about 3 tablespoons drippings from skillet into blender. Discard remaining drippings. Add parsley, ginger, poultry seasoning, salt, pepper and allspice to meat mixture. Process until almost smooth. Pour into a 3-cup crock or bowl. Refrigerate 3 to 4 hours before serving. Makes about 3 cups.

Velvety Chicken Liver Pâté and Appetizer Puffs, page 77 with Creamed Antipasto Filling, page 81

Clock-Watcher Deviled Pâté

Using prepared spreads saves preparation time.

1 (.25-oz.) envelope unflavored gelatin
1 cup beef broth or bouillon
1 (4-3/4-oz.) can liverwurst spread
1 (4-3/4-oz.) can deviled ham spread
1/4 cup dairy sour cream

1 teaspoon grated onion
1 teaspoon lemon juice
Watercress sprigs for garnish
Crackers

In a small saucepan, add gelatin to broth or bouillon. Let stand 3 to 4 minutes to soften. Stir over low heat until dissolved; remove from heat. Pour 1/2 dissolved gelatin mixture into bottom of a 3-cup decorative mold or bowl. Reserve remaining gelatin mixture at room temperature. Refrigerate mold or bowl until gelatin mixture mounds when dropped from a spoon, 30 to 45 minutes. Surface must be sticky. Into reserved unchilled gelatin mixture, stir liverwurst spread, deviled ham spread, sour cream, grated onion and lemon juice until thoroughly combined. Pour over chilled gelatin in mold or bowl. Refrigerate until firm, 4 to 6 hours. To unmold, dip mold to depth of contents in and out of warm water 3 or 4 times. Invert onto a platter; remove mold. Garnish with watercress sprigs. Serve with crackers. Makes 2-1/2 cups.

Chicken Liver Terrine

You can slice this creamy and rich tasting pâté.

4 or 5 slices bacon
2 eggs
1 onion, quartered
1 garlic clove, quartered
1 lb. chicken livers
3 tablespoons all-purpose flour

1 teaspoon salt
1/4 teaspoon pepper
1/4 teaspoon ground allspice
1 cup whipping cream
Crackers or Melba toast

Line an 8'' x 4'' loaf pan with slices of bacon, letting bacon ends extend over side; set aside. Preheat oven to 325°F (165°C). In blender, combine eggs, onion and garlic. Blend until almost smooth. Add chicken livers, flour, salt, pepper, allspice and cream. Blend until smooth. Pour into bacon-lined pan; bring bacon over top of meat mixture. Cover with foil. Set loaf pan in a 13'' x 9'' baking pan. Pour about 1 inch boiling water into outer pan. Bake 1-1/2 hours in preheated oven until firm. Cool on a rack 1 hour. Refrigerate 6 hours or overnight. Invert onto a platter; remove pan. Cut into 14 to 16 slices; cut each slice in half. Serve with crackers or Melba toast. Makes one 8'' x 4'' loaf or 28 to 36 appetizer servings.

Bacon used to line a terrine provides flavor and moisture to pâtes during the baking process.

Potted Pork & Bacon

Two pork meats and a blend of herbs flavor this spread.

1/2 lb. boneless lean pork, diced
1/2 lb. bacon, diced
1 cup water
1 cup dry white wine
1 bay leaf

1 teaspoon dried thyme leaves
1 garlic clove, minced
1/4 teaspoon salt
1/8 teaspoon pepper
Crackers or Melba toast

In a large saucepan, combine all ingredients except crackers or toast. Bring to a boil. Simmer uncovered, about 1-1/2 hours until liquid is reduced to about 1 cup. Pour off drippings through a strainer, reserving liquid. Discard bay leaf. Refrigerate reserved liquid and meat mixture, about 30 minutes. When cool, remove most of fat. Pour liquid into blender or food processor. Add meat mixture; process until almost smooth. Spoon into a small crock or jar. Cover and refrigerate 3 to 4 hours. Serve with crackers or Melba toast. Makes about 1 cup.

Rillettes of Pork

French rillettes are more coarse than most pâtés.

3 to 3-1/2 lbs. boned pork shoulder
1 carrot, coarsely chopped
1 garlic clove, crushed
1/4 cup water
1/2 teaspoon dried sage

1 teaspoon salt
1/4 teaspoon pepper
Pinch ground allspice
French bread, cut or torn in thick pieces

Cut pork into 1/2-inch cubes, using fat and lean meat. Place in a 3-quart casserole dish. Add carrot. In a small bowl, combine garlic, water, sage, salt, pepper and allspice. Pour over pork and carrot. Cover tightly with lid or foil. Place in cold oven. Turn oven temperature control to 275°F (135°C). Bake 4 to 5 hours until meat is very tender. Strain and reserve drippings. Use 2 forks to shred cooked meat. Spoon shredded meat and cooked carrot into a 4-cup bowl or crock; pack meat mixture down with back of spoon. Pour reserved drippings over top, covering meat. Refrigerate 6 hours or overnight. Scrape excess fat from top of meat mixture. Serve cold on French bread. Makes about 4 cups.

Short-Cut Pâté

No one will guess this excellent blend of flavors took so little preparation time.

1/2 lb. liverwurst, cut in 6 pieces
2 tablespoons dry white wine
1 teaspoon dried minced onion
1/4 teaspoon garlic salt

1/4 teaspoon dried basil leaves
1/4 cup butter, melted
French bread, sliced, or crackers

In blender or food processor, combine liverwurst, wine, onion, garlic salt, basil and butter. Process until smooth. Spoon into a small bowl or crock. Refrigerate 30 minutes to chill or serve at room temperature with French bread or crackers. Makes about 1-1/4 cups.

Caviar-Crowned Mold

Use a pedestal cake stand or footed sandwich plate to present this spectacular-looking mold.

1 cup cottage cheese	3 hard-cooked eggs
1 cup dairy sour cream	1 (2-oz.) jar red or black caviar
1 teaspoon lemon juice	3 green onions, finely chopped
1 teaspoon Worcestershire sauce	3 slices lemon
1/4 teaspoon seasoned salt	Pumpernickel bread or rye bread,
1 (.25-oz.) envelope unflavored gelatin	thinly sliced
1/4 cup chilled dry white wine	

In blender or food processor, combine cottage cheese, sour cream, lemon juice, Worcestershire sauce and seasoned salt. Process until smooth, 10 to 20 seconds. In a small saucepan, sprinkle gelatin over wine; let stand 3 to 4 minutes to soften. Stir over low heat until gelatin dissolves. Gradually stir dissolved gelatin mixture into cottage cheese mixture. Pour into a 9- or 10-inch quiche pan or springform pan. Refrigerate until firm, 4 to 6 hours. Finely chop hard-cooked eggs; set aside. Invert firmly set mold onto a large round platter; remove pan. Spoon caviar in a 1-inch ring around outer edge on top of mold. Spoon chopped eggs in a 1-1/2-inch ring inside caviar ring. Cover remaining surface with chopped onions. Garnish center with lemon slices. Serve as spread with pumpernickel bread or rye bread. Makes 35 to 40 appetizer servings.

Guacamole Mold   Photo on pages 2 and 3.

Lemon juice keeps the avocado from turning dark.

1 (.25-oz.) envelope unflavored gelatin	2 teaspoons grated onion
1/4 cup cold water	1 teaspoon seasoned salt
1 cup chicken broth or bouillon	1/2 teaspoon chili powder
2 large ripe avocados	2 tablespoons canned diced green chilies
2 tablespoons lemon juice	Dash hot pepper sauce
1/2 cup dairy sour cream	Tortilla chips or corn chips

In a small bowl, stir gelatin into cold water. Let stand 3 to 4 minutes to soften. In a small saucepan, bring chicken broth or bouillon to a boil. Stir into gelatin mixture until dissolved; set aside. In a medium bowl, mash avocados. Stir in lemon juice, sour cream, grated onion, seasoned salt, chili powder, green chilies and hot pepper sauce. Slowly stir in dissolved gelatin mixture until evenly distributed. Pour into a 4-cup mold. Refrigerate until firm, 4 to 6 hours. To unmold, dip mold to depth of contents in and out of warm water 3 or 4 times. Invert onto a small platter or tray; remove mold. Serve with tortilla chips or corn chips. Makes about 4 cups.

Caviar-Crowned Mold

Roquefort Mold

Stretch your budget by using blue cheese instead of Roquefort.

1 (.25-oz.) envelope unflavored gelatin
1/4 cup cold water
1 (3-oz.) pkg. cream cheese,
 room temperature
4 oz. Roquefort cheese, crumbled

1 teaspoon Dijon-style mustard
1 teaspoon grated onion
1/2 cup whipping cream
Crackers

In a small saucepan, sprinkle gelatin over cold water. Let stand 3 to 4 minutes to soften. Stir over very low heat until dissolved; set aside. In a medium bowl, combine cream cheese and Roquefort cheese. Beat with electric mixer until light and fluffy. Stir in mustard, onion and dissolved gelatin. In a small bowl, beat cream until stiff peaks form. Fold into cheese mixture. Spoon into a 3- or 4-cup mold. Refrigerate 4 to 6 hours. To unmold, dip mold to depth of contents in and out of warm water 3 or 4 times. Invert onto a small platter; remove mold. Serve with crackers. Makes about 2-1/2 cups.

Aloha Loaf   Photo on pages 30 and 31.

Chill this soft festive loaf thoroughly to make it easy to slice.

2 cups finely grated Cheddar cheese
 (8 oz.)
1/4 cup dairy sour cream
1/4 cup minced green pepper
Dash hot pepper sauce
2 tablespoons minced parsley
2 cups ground cooked ham
1 (8-1/4-oz.) can crushed pineapple,
 well drained

1 (3-oz.) pkg. cream cheese,
 room temperature
1 tablespoon finely chopped crystallized
 ginger
Parsley sprigs for garnish
Kumquats for garnish
Crackers or Melba toast

Line a 9" x 5" loaf pan with waxed paper; set aside. In a small bowl, combine Cheddar cheese, sour cream, green pepper and hot pepper sauce. Spread on bottom of lined pan. Sprinkle minced parsley over top; lightly press into Cheddar cheese mixture. Refrigerate at least 2 hours. In a medium bowl, combine ham, pineapple, cream cheese and ginger. Spread over chilled Cheddar cheese mixture. Refrigerate at least 2 hours. At serving time, invert loaf onto a serving dish; remove loaf pan and waxed paper. Garnish with parsley sprigs and kumquats. Cut into 16 to 18 slices; cut each slice in half. Serve cold with crackers or Melba toast. Makes one 9" x 5" loaf or 32 to 36 appetizer servings.

Small bowls make handy and inexpensive molds if you don't have decorative molds.

Egg & Caviar Strata

Use a small round bowl in place of the small gelatin mold.

2 tablespoons dry white wine
2 tablespoons lemon juice
1 (.25-oz.) envelope unflavored gelatin
4 hard-cooked eggs
1 cup mayonnaise

1 teaspoon anchovy paste
1 tablespoon chopped parsley
1 (2-oz.) jar lumpfish caviar
1 teaspoon Worcestershire sauce
Pumpernickel bread, thinly sliced

In a small saucepan, combine wine and lemon juice. Sprinkle gelatin over wine mixture. Let stand 3 to 4 minutes to soften. Stir over very low heat until gelatin dissolves. Chop hard-cooked eggs; set aside. Spoon mayonnaise into a medium bowl. Gradually stir hot gelatin mixture into mayonnaise. Reserve half of mayonnaise mixture at room temperature. Pour remaining mayonnaise mixture into a small bowl. Stir in chopped eggs, anchovy paste and chopped parsley. Pour into a 3-cup mold or bowl; refrigerate 30 to 45 minutes until partially set and sticky on top. Stir caviar and Worcestershire sauce into reserved mayonnaise mixture. Spoon caviar mixture over sticky surface of egg mixture in mold. Refrigerate until firm, 4 to 6 hours. To unmold, dip mold to depth of contents in and out of warm water 3 or 4 times. Invert onto a small round platter; remove mold. Spread on pumpernickel bread. Makes 3 cups.

Caviar Pie

Refrigerate several hours to let both layers chill thoroughly.

6 eggs
1/4 cup butter, room temperature
1 teaspoon prepared mustard
1/4 teaspoon salt
1/8 teaspoon pepper
1 teaspoon vinegar
1/2 cup chopped green onions
1 cup dairy sour cream

1 (3-oz.) pkg. cream cheese,
  room temperature
2 tablespoons chopped pimiento
1 (2-oz.) jar lumpfish caviar
Lemon slices
Pimiento strips
Rye bread or pumpernickel bread,
  thinly sliced

Hard-cook eggs; peel and quarter eggs as soon as cool enough to handle comfortably. While still warm, combine quartered eggs, butter, mustard, salt, pepper and vinegar in blender or food processor. Process until smooth, 15 to 30 seconds. Spread over bottom of an 8-inch springform pan. Sprinkle evenly with onions. Refrigerate at least 1 hour. In a small bowl, stir sour cream and cream cheese until smooth. Stir in chopped pimiento. Spread over chilled egg mixture. Refrigerate 1 hour longer. Gently spoon caviar evenly over cream cheese mixture. Garnish with lemon slices and pimiento strips. Remove side of pan. Cut pie into 35 to 40 small wedges. Spread on thinly sliced rye bread or pumpernickel bread. Makes one 8-inch pie or 35 to 40 appetizer servings.

Calico Mold

Get your Mexican party off to a good start with this spicy mold.

1 (.25-oz.) envelope unflavored gelatin	2 tablespoons finely chopped pimiento
1 cup cold water	2 tablespoons finely chopped ripe olives
1 cup dairy sour cream	1 tablespoon finely chopped onion
2 cups finely grated sharp Cheddar cheese (8 oz.)	Crackers or tortilla chips
1 (4-oz.) can diced green chilies, drained	

In a small saucepan, sprinkle gelatin over cold water. Let stand 3 or 4 minutes to soften. Stir over low heat until gelatin dissolves; set aside. In a medium bowl, combine sour cream and Cheddar cheese. Stir in chilies, pimiento, olives and onion. Gradually stir in dissolved gelatin. Refrigerate until mixture mounds when dropped from a spoon, 30 to 45 minutes. Stir to evenly distribute ingredients; spoon into a 4-cup fluted mold. Refrigerate until firm, 4 to 6 hours. To unmold, dip mold to depth of contents in and out of warm water 3 or 4 times. Invert onto a small platter or tray; remove mold. To serve, spread on crackers or tortilla chips. Makes about 4 cups.

Ham & Eggs in Aspic   Photo on pages 2 and 3.

Egg cups hold about 4-ounces liquid and make a nice size serving.

2 (.25-oz.) envelopes unflavored gelatin	1 green onion
3 cups chicken bouillon or broth	1 tablespoon chopped pimiento
2 tablespoons white wine	3 hard-cooked eggs
1 tablespoon lemon juice	1/2 cup finely chopped ham

In a small saucepan, sprinkle gelatin over 1 cup bouillon or broth to soften. Stir oven low heat until gelatin dissolves. Stir in remaining bouillon or broth, wine and lemon juice. Spoon about 1 tablespoon gelatin mixture into each of 6 egg-shaped molds or small custard cups. Place in freezer until partially set, 5 to 10 minutes. Refrigerate remaining mixture. Cut onion tops into 12 very thin strips about 2 inches long. Arrange 2 onion strips and 2 or 3 pieces pimiento on partially set gelatin in each egg cup. Refrigerate until partially set, 15 to 30 minutes. Cut eggs in half lengthwise. Place 1/2 egg, cut-side down, on partially set gelatin in each cup. Spoon 2 tablespoons reserved refrigerated gelatin over each egg; refrigerate 15 to 20 minutes until partially set. Sprinkle ham evenly in cups. Fill cups with reserved gelatin mixture. Pour remaining reserved gelatin into a 9'' x 5'' loaf pan. Refrigerate both mixtures until firm, 2 to 4 hours. Arrange lettuce leaves on 6 salad plates. Invert each egg mold onto a lettuce-lined plate; remove egg cup or custard mold. Finely chop remaining gelatin; arrange on lettuce around eggs. Makes 6 servings.

How to Make Calico Mold

1/Stir green chilies, pimiento and ripe olives into sour cream and Cheddar cheese mixture before adding dissolved gelatin.

2/Refrigerate gelatin mixture until partially set, 1 to 1-1/2 hours. Stir, then spoon into a 4-cup mold.

Tuna Mousse

It's pretty in a ring mold with cherry tomatoes in the center.

1/4 cup dry white wine	1/2 teaspoon dried marjoram leaves
2 (.25-oz.) envelopes unflavored gelatin	1/4 cup mayonnaise
1 cup chicken broth or bouillon	2 (6-1/2-oz.) cans tuna, drained
1/3 cup chopped celery	1 cup half-and-half
2 green onions, chopped	2 egg whites
1/4 teaspoon salt	5 or 6 lettuce leaves
2 tablespoons sweet pickle relish, drained	Crackers

Pour wine into a small saucepan. Sprinkle gelatin over wine; let stand 3 to 4 minutes to soften. Add chicken broth or bouillon. Stir over very low heat 3 to 4 minutes until gelatin dissolves; set aside. In blender or food processor, combine celery, onions, salt, sweet pickle relish, marjoram and mayonnaise. Process 2 to 10 seconds. Mixture will not be pureed. Add dissolved gelatin mixture, tuna and half-and-half. Process 2 to 5 seconds to break up tuna chunks. In a large bowl, beat egg whites until stiff but not dry. Fold tuna mixture into beaten egg whites. Spoon into a 5-cup mold. Refrigerate until firm, 4 to 6 hours. Arrange lettuce leaves around edge of a medium, round platter or tray. To unmold, dip mold to depth of contents in and out of warm water 3 or 4 times. Invert onto lettuce-lined platter or tray; remove mold. Serve as a spread with crackers. Makes 5 cups.

Upside-Down Chili Ring

Serve this baked custard-like spread with crackers or Melba toast at a fireside get-together.

1/4 cup fine dry breadcrumbs
1 cup finely grated Cheddar cheese
  (4 oz.)
1 (4-oz.) can diced green chilies,
  well drained
3 eggs

1 cup half-and-half
1/2 cup dairy sour cream
1/4 cup grated Parmesan cheese (1 oz.)
1 teaspoon minced parsley
1/4 teaspoon salt
1/4 teaspoon dried oregano leaves, crushed

Grease a 5-cup ring mold. Sprinkle bottom and about 1 inch up side of mold with breadcrumbs. Repeat with Cheddar cheese and green chilies; set aside. Preheat oven to 350°F (175°C). In a medium bowl, beat eggs slightly. Stir in half-and-half, sour cream, Parmesan cheese, parsley, salt and oregano. Carefully pour into lined ring mold. Bake 30 to 40 minutes in preheated oven until mixture is firm. Run a small spatula around side of mold. Invert onto a small platter; remove mold. Serve warm as a spread. Makes 5 cups.

Potted Rumaki Spread

Traditional rumaki has chicken livers and water chestnuts rolled in bacon strips.

4 slices bacon, diced
1/2 lb. chicken livers
1 green onion, chopped
1 tablespoon soy sauce
1/8 teaspoon garlic salt
1 tablespoon white wine vinegar

1/2 teaspoon Dijon-style mustard
2 tablespoons butter, melted
1 (6-oz.) can water chestnuts, drained,
  finely chopped
Crackers

In a medium skillet, cook bacon over medium heat until most of fat is removed but bacon is still soft. Pat chicken livers dry with paper towels. Add livers and onion to bacon; sauté over low heat until livers are lightly browned. Drain on paper towels. In blender, combine cooked bacon, sautéed livers and onion, soy sauce, garlic salt, vinegar, mustard and butter. Blend 3 to 10 seconds until well mixed, but not smooth. Spoon into a small crock or bowl. Stir in water chestnuts. Refrigerate at least 1 hour. Use as a spread for crackers. Makes about 1-1/3 cups.

Sauté chicken livers only until the pink color disappears. Over-cooked livers are dry and tough.

Spicy Beef Ball

Make this spicy ball the night before to let the flavors blend.

1 (8-oz.) pkg. cream cheese,
  room temperature
1/4 cup mayonnaise
2 green onions, finely chopped
1-1/2 teaspoons prepared mustard
1-1/2 teaspoons prepared horseradish

1/8 teaspoon garlic salt
1 (3-oz.) pkg. thinly sliced corned beef
  or pastrami
Pumpernickel bread or party rye bread,
  thinly sliced

In a medium bowl, beat cream cheese and mayonnaise until smooth. Stir in onions, mustard, horseradish and garlic salt. Finely chop corned beef or pastrami; stir into cream cheese mixture. Shape into a 4-inch ball. Refrigerate 3 to 4 hours until firm. Serve with thinly sliced pumpernickel or party rye bread. Makes about 2 cups.

Pickled Chili Spread

You'll be pleasantly surprised at the sweet yet spicy flavor.

1/4 cup sugar
1/4 cup white wine vinegar
1/2 teaspoon salt
1/2 teaspoon dill seeds
1/2 teaspoon mustard seeds
1 garlic clove, minced

1 (7-oz.) can diced green chilies,
  drained
1 (8-oz.) pkg. cream cheese,
  room temperature
Crackers or corn chips

In a small saucepan, combine sugar, vinegar, salt, dill seeds, mustard seeds and garlic. Bring to a boil. Cook and stir until sugar dissolves, 2 to 3 minutes. Stir in chilies. Cook and stir 2 to 3 minutes longer. Turn into a small bowl. Cover and refrigerate 6 hours or overnight. Drain, pressing mixture with back of a spoon to remove moisture. In a medium bowl, stir cream cheese to soften. Stir in drained chili mixture. Serve with crackers or corn chips. Makes 2 cups.

Finely chop meats or vegetables before including them in spreads for crackers or bread.

Party-Time Spread

Add more hot pepper sauce if you like a spicier mixture.

2 hard-cooked eggs
1 large avocado
1/2 lb. cooked shrimp, shelled,
  finely chopped
2 green onions, finely chopped
1 tablespoon lemon juice

1/4 teaspoon salt
1/4 teaspoon seasoned salt
1/4 teaspoon dried tarragon leaves
3 or 4 drops hot pepper sauce
Melba toast or crackers

Finely chop hard-cooked eggs; set aside. Finely chop avocado. In a medium bowl, combine chopped eggs, chopped avocado, shrimp, onions, lemon juice, salt, seasoned salt, tarragon and hot pepper sauce. Spoon into a 2- or 3-cup decorative bowl or crock. Refrigerate 6 hours or overnight. Serve cold with Melba toast or crackers. Makes 2 cups.

Moussaka Spread

This makes an excellent filling for pita bread.

1 medium eggplant
2 tablespoons olive oil or vegetable oil
1 cup chopped cooked lamb or beef
1 (6-oz.) can tomato paste
1 garlic clove, crushed
1 tablespoon chopped parsley

1/2 teaspoon salt
1/4 teaspoon pepper
1/8 teaspoon ground nutmeg
1/2 cup plain yogurt
1/4 cup grated Parmesan cheese (1 oz.)
Sesame crackers or toasted pita bread

Preheat oven to 400°F (205°C). Prick skin of eggplant several times with a fork. Place punctured eggplant in a shallow 9-inch square baking pan. Bake about 1 hour in preheated oven until eggplant collapses. Cool, peel and chop eggplant. In blender or food processor, combine chopped eggplant, oil, lamb or beef, tomato paste, garlic, parsley, salt, pepper and nutmeg. Process 3 to 10 seconds until blended. Mixture will not be smooth. Stir in yogurt. Spoon mixture into a 3- to 4-cup baking dish; sprinkle with Parmesan cheese. Reduce oven heat to 350°F (175°C). Bake casserole about 30 minutes until mixture bubbles. If serving at a later time, refrigerate until 35 minutes before serving. Heat mixture as directed above for 35 minutes. Serve hot on sesame crackers or toasted pita bread. Makes 3 cups.

Calcutta Chicken Spread

Crystallized ginger is ginger root in confection form.

1/2 cup mayonnaise
1/2 cup dairy sour cream
1 tablespoon minced crystallized ginger
2 teaspoons soy sauce
1 tablespoon minced green onion

1 (8-1/2-oz.) can water chestnuts,
   drained, chopped
1 cup finely chopped cooked chicken
Sesame crackers

In a medium bowl, combine mayonnaise, sour cream, ginger, soy sauce and onion. Stir in water chestnuts and chicken. Serve with sesame crackers. Makes about 2 cups.

Pineapple-Cheese Spread

Serve cold with Melba toast or follow the variation below.

2 cups grated sharp Cheddar cheese
   (8 oz.)
1 (8-oz.) can crushed pineapple, drained
1/4 cup finely chopped green pepper

2 tablespoons minced chives
1 teaspoon soy sauce
1/2 cup chopped pecans
1/4 cup mayonnaise

In a medium bowl, combine Cheddar cheese, pineapple, green pepper, chives, soy sauce, pecans and mayonnaise. Refrigerate 2 to 3 hours; serve cold. Makes 2 cups.

Variation

To serve hot, spread about 2 tablespoons pineapple-cheese mixture on each of 16 lightly toasted English muffin halves. Broil until bubbly. Cut each muffin half into 4 wedges; serve immediately. Makes about 64 appetizer servings.

Sampan Spread

Cut the pita bread into thin wedges and arrange around bowl of spread.

4 hard-cooked eggs
1/4 cup dairy sour cream
1/4 cup mayonnaise
2 teaspoons curry powder

1/4 teaspoon salt
1/4 cup chutney
1/4 cup finely chopped peanuts
Pita bread or pumpernickel bread

Chop hard-cooked eggs. In a medium bowl, combine chopped hard-cooked eggs, sour cream, mayonnaise, curry powder and salt. Remove fruit from chutney; chop fine. Add chopped fruit and chutney syrup to egg mixture. Spoon into a small serving bowl. Sprinkle peanuts over top. Serve with pita bread or pumpernickel bread. Makes 1-3/4 cups.

Chutney-Cheese Spread

Spicy but not overpowering. One of our favorites.

1 cup grated Cheddar cheese (4 oz.)
1 (3-oz.) pkg. cream cheese,
  room temperature
1/4 cup chutney

2 green onions, minced
1/4 teaspoon ground ginger
1/4 teaspoon salt
Sesame crackers

In a medium bowl, combine Cheddar cheese and cream cheese. Remove fruit from chutney; chop fine. Add chopped fruit and chutney syrup to cheese mixture. Stir in onions, ginger and salt. Chill 6 hours or overnight to blend flavors. Serve with sesame crackers. Makes 1 cup.

King Kamehameha Spread

Ideal appetizer for any Hawaiian party. Spread on wheat crackers or whole-wheat bread.

1 (1-1/4-oz.) pkg. blue cheese, crumbled
1 (8-oz.) pkg. cream cheese,
  room temperature
1 tablespoon finely chopped crystallized
  ginger

1/4 cup finely chopped toasted
  macadamia nuts or almonds
1 (8-oz.) can crushed pineapple, drained

In a small bowl, stir blue cheese and cream cheese until smooth. Stir in ginger, nuts and pineapple. Makes 1-1/2 cups.

How to Make Chutney-Cheese Spread

1/Before using chutney in a spread or dip, remove fruit from sauce. Chop fruit into small pieces.

2/Stir chopped fruit and chutney sauce into cheese mixture. Stir in green onions and seasonings.

Curry Spread

You'll enjoy the delightful flavor with sesame crackers or crisp toast.

1 (8-oz.) pkg. cream cheese, room temperature	1/2 cup finely chopped peanuts
1/4 cup dairy sour cream	1/2 cup finely chopped raisins
2 teaspoons curry powder	2 slices bacon, cooked crisp, crumbled
1/4 teaspoon garlic salt	2 tablespoons finely chopped green onions

In a medium bowl, combine cream cheese, sour cream, curry powder and garlic salt, stirring until smooth. Stir in peanuts, raisins and bacon. Spoon into a medium serving bowl; sprinkle evenly with onions. Makes about 2 cups.

Supreme Cream Cheese & Lox

Lox is a deliciously brined and thinly sliced smoked salmon.

1 (8-oz.) pkg. cream cheese,
   room temperature
1 tablespoon lemon juice
1/8 teaspoon pepper
2 tablespoons finely chopped
   watercress leaves

1/4 lb. smoked salmon, finely chopped
2 tablespoons butter, melted
1/2 lb. loaf pumpernickel bread,
   thinly sliced
Bagels

In a medium bowl, beat cream cheese, lemon juice and pepper until smooth. Stir in watercress, salmon and butter. Spoon into a 2- or 3-cup mold or bowl. Refrigerate about 4 hours until firm. Invert mold onto a medium tray; remove mold. Serve with thin slices of pumpernickel bread or bagels. Makes 1-1/2 cups.

Deviled Ham & Cheese

It takes about five minutes to prepare this deliciously tangy spread.

2 cups grated Cheddar cheese (8 oz.)
1 (4-1/2-oz.) can deviled ham spread
1/3 cup mayonnaise
2 teaspoons Dijon-style mustard

1 teaspoon prepared horseradish
Pumpernickel bread or rye bread,
   thinly sliced

In a medium bowl, combine Cheddar cheese, ham spread, mayonnaise, mustard and horseradish. Spoon into a small crock or mound on a saucer. Refrigerate 2 to 3 hours and serve cold as a spread with pumpernickel or rye bread. To serve hot, preheat broiler if necessary. Spread mixture on bread slices and broil 5 to 8 inches from heating element until bubbly; serve hot. Makes about 2 cups.

Roquefort Crock

Piquant cheese and mustard flavors are perfect to serve with fresh apples or pears.

1/4 lb. Roquefort cheese, crumbled
1 (3-oz.) pkg. cream cheese,
   room temperature
1 teaspoon Dijon-style mustard

1/2 cup whipping cream
Crackers
2 red-skinned apples or 2 pears, sliced

In a small bowl, beat Roquefort cheese and cream cheese until smooth. Beat in mustard. In another small bowl, whip cream until stiff but not dry. Fold whipped cream into cheese mixture. Pack into a 12-ounce jar or crock. Refrigerate 6 hours or overnight. Serve with crackers, apple slices or pear slices. Makes 1-1/2 cups.

Dip Collection

Dips are synonymous with appetizers. Present dips dramatically in your grandmother's cut glass bon bon dish, a soup bowl from your dinnerware set, in a small earthenware crock or a regular dip bowl. Put the filled container on a cake plate, cutting board or meat platter. Surround the dip with chips, crackers or bite-size vegetable pieces.

On a cold winter's night, what could give more comforting warmth than a hot dip? Hot appetizers beg to be tried and are a wise choice for busy entertainers. They can be prepared at least several hours or even one or two days ahead. Keep them refrigerated until about 30 minutes before serving. Heat them on the stove, in your fondue pot or in a slow-cooker, then keep them hot in these two containers or on an electric hot tray. There are also some good looking glazed earthenware pots or clay pots available that heat slowly but hold the heat a long time. All of these containers will keep you from running back and forth to the kitchen to reheat the dip. Be sure to keep food below the boiling point to avoid drying out or having it stick to the pan.

Dips should be nutritious as well as interesting. Both requirements are met in robust Cheese Dunk made with cottage, Cheddar and Roquefort cheeses, horseradish and mustard. If guests prefer a low-calorie dip, prepare a trio of Fresh Herb Dip, Low-Calorie Dip and Calorie Counter's Blue Cheese Dip. Fresh herbs and yogurt are combined in traditional Salmon Rémoulade Dip, making this another low-calorie offering.

A sixteenth-century cookbook admonished diners to wash their hands where others could see and know that the fingers dipped in the common dish were clean. Luckily, today's diners use something besides fingers as dippers. Serve one or more of the following, cutting them large enough so fingers are spared the heat of the dip:

- Bread slices, sticks or chunks including Armenian cracker bread, French bread, pita bread, party rye, melba toast and crisp rye toast.
- Crackers, potato chips, tortilla chips and pretzels.
- Fresh fruits such as apples and pears.
- Fully cooked meat cubes.
- Marinated or pickled vegetables.
- Vegetable sticks, slices, chunks or flowerets made from carrots, asparagus, broccoli, cauliflower, celery, cucumbers, jicama, onions, turnips, zucchini, chili or bell peppers.

Green Goddess Dip

Serve fresh, raw vegetables or corn chips as dippers.

8 flat anchovy fillets, finely chopped
1 (3-oz.) pkg. cream cheese,
  room temperature
1 cup dairy sour cream
1 garlic clove, minced
1/4 cup finely chopped green onions

1/4 cup minced parsley
1/2 teaspoon dried tarragon leaves,
  crushed
1/4 teaspoon pepper
1 tablespoon vinegar

In a small bowl, stir anchovies into cream cheese. Stir in remaining ingredients. Makes 1-1/2 cups.

Fresh Herb Dip

Everyone will enjoy this dieter's delight.

1 tablespoon minced chives
1 tablespoon minced tarragon
1 tablespoon minced watercress
1 garlic clove, crushed
1/4 teaspoon salt
1/8 teaspoon pepper
1/2 cup plain yogurt

1/2 cup dairy sour cream
2 carrots, peeled, cut in thin sticks
2 celery stalks, cut in thin sticks
1/3 lb. broccoli, cut in flowerets
1/2 small head cauliflower,
  cut in flowerets

In a small bowl, combine chives, tarragon, watercress, garlic, salt and pepper. Stir in yogurt and sour cream. Serve with carrot sticks, celery sticks, broccoli flowerets and cauliflowerets. Makes about 1 cup.

Salmon Rémoulade Dip

Reminiscent of old New Orleans, rémoulade is usually a sauce for cold fish and shellfish.

1 cup dairy sour cream
1 garlic clove, crushed
1 teaspoon prepared mustard
1/2 teaspoon dried tarragon leaves,
  crushed
1 tablespoon minced parsley

1 teaspoon lemon juice
1 hard-cooked egg, finely chopped
1 (7-3/4-oz.) can salmon, drained,
  flaked
Raw vegetable sticks and flowerets or
  potato chips for dipping

In a medium bowl, combine sour cream, garlic, mustard, tarragon, parsley and lemon juice. Stir in egg and salmon. Spoon into a serving bowl. Refrigerate until served. Serve with variety of vegetable sticks and flowerets or potato chips for dipping. Makes 1-3/4 cups.

Green Goddess Dip with Fresh Vegetable Dippers

Vegetable Dip

Patient, slow addition of the oil will give you a thick, creamy dip.

1/4 cup chopped watercress
1 tablespoon chopped chives
1/2 teaspoon dried tarragon leaves
3 flat anchovy fillets, chopped
2 teaspoons drained capers
2 tablespoons vegetable oil
1 teaspoon Dijon-style mustard

1 tablespoon lemon juice
1/8 teaspoon salt
1 egg
1-1/4 cups vegetable oil
2 carrots, peeled, cut in sticks
2 celery stalks, cut in thin sticks
1 medium turnip, peeled, sliced

In blender or food processor, combine watercress, chives, tarragon, anchovy fillets and capers. Process until finely minced. Add 2 tablespoons oil, mustard, lemon juice, salt and egg. Process until mixture thickens, 20 to 30 seconds. Continue processing while slowly drizzling 1-1/4 cups oil into watercress mixture. Process until thickened, about 10 seconds. Serve with carrot sticks, celery sticks and turnip slices. Makes 1-3/4 cups.

Calorie Counter's Blue Cheese Dip

Quick as a wink to prepare.

2 cups plain yogurt
4 oz. blue cheese, crumbled
1 teaspoon Worcestershire sauce
1 tablespoon minced chives

1/8 teaspoon pepper
Raw vegetable sticks and flowerets for
 dipping

In a medium bowl, combine yogurt, blue cheese, Worcestershire sauce, chives and pepper, stirring to distribute. Serve with raw fresh vegetable dippers. Makes 2-1/4 cups.

You don't have to ruin your diet with dips. Try one of our yogurt-based creations with raw vegetables instead of chips and crackers.

How to Make Vegetable Dip

1/Chop watercress, chives and anchovies for ease in measuring. Measure other ingredients.

2/Green color comes from watercress and chives. Serve with fresh vegetable dippers.

Low Calorie Dip

Serve this delectable dip with raw fresh vegetables.

2 cups low fat cottage cheese
1 teaspoon paprika
1 tablespoon prepared horseradish
1 garlic clove, crushed

1 teaspoon dried dill weed
1/2 teaspoon salt
1/4 teaspoon dry mustard

In blender or food processor, combine all ingredients. Process until nearly smooth. Spoon into a medium serving bowl. Makes 1-3/4 cups.

If you don't have a fondue pot, warm and serve dips in your electric slow cooker.

Cheese Dunk

Drain the cottage cheese so your dip will be thick.

2 cups cottage cheese
1 cup grated sharp Cheddar cheese (4 oz.)
2 oz. Roquefort cheese or blue cheese,
    crumbled
3 tablespoons mayonnaise
2 tablespoons prepared horseradish

1 tablespoon prepared mustard
3 green onions, finely chopped
1/4 teaspoon salt
1/8 teaspoon pepper
2 apples, sliced
2 pears, sliced

Drain cottage cheese. In a medium bowl, combine drained cottage cheese, Cheddar cheese, Roquefort cheese, mayonnaise, horseradish, mustard, onions, salt and pepper, stirring to blend ingredients. Spoon into a medium serving bowl. Serve with apples, pears and potato chips for dipping. Makes about 3 cups.

Bacon & Avocado Dip

Make this dip at least one hour before your guests arrive.

3 slices bacon
2 ripe avocados
1 tablespoon lemon juice
2 green onions, chopped
1/4 teaspoon salt

1 small tomato, peeled, seeded, chopped
2 canned green chili peppers, seeded,
    chopped
Tortilla chips or corn chips for dippers

In a medium skillet, cook bacon until crisp; drain on paper towels. Crumble and set aside to cool. In a medium bowl, use a fork to mash avocados. Stir in lemon juice, onions, salt, tomato, chili peppers and crumbled bacon. Cover and refrigerate 1 to 2 hours. Serve with tortilla chips or corn chips for dippers. Makes about 2 cups.

How to Make Cheese Dunk

1/Drain cottage cheese in a sieve 15 to 20 minutes before combining with other ingredients.

2/Serve this chunky 3-cheese dip with fresh apple slices and fresh pear slices.

Yogacado Dip

Avocados and yogurt are a nice combination in this smooth tangy dip.

2 ripe avocados, cut in large pieces
1/2 cup plain yogurt
1/2 teaspoon chili powder
1 teaspoon lemon juice

1 garlic clove, crushed
1/4 teaspoon salt
Variety of raw fresh vegetables or
   corn chips for dippers

In blender, combine avocado pieces, yogurt, chili powder, lemon juice, garlic and salt. Blend until smooth. Spoon into a small serving bowl. Serve chilled or at room temperature with raw fresh vegetables or corn chips for dippers. Makes 1-1/2 cups.

Guacamole

You'll get a smoother dip if you process the avocado in your blender.

1 large ripe avocado
2 teaspoons lemon juice
1/4 teaspoon salt
1 canned California green chili,
   finely chopped
1/2 teaspoon Worcestershire sauce

1 teaspoon grated onion
3 or 4 drops hot pepper sauce
1 garlic clove, crushed
1 small tomato, chopped, if desired
Corn chips or tortilla chips for dipping

In a small bowl, use a fork to mash avocado. Stir in lemon juice, salt, green chili, Worcestershire sauce, onion, hot pepper sauce, garlic and tomato, if desired. Serve with corn chips or tortilla chips for dipping. Makes about 3/4 cup.

Dilled Cucumber & Salmon

Cucumber is sprinkled with salt to remove excess liquid.

1 large cucumber
1 teaspoon salt
1 cup dairy sour cream
1/2 cup mayonnaise
1/4 teaspoon pepper
1/4 teaspoon seasoned salt

2 teaspoons dried dill weed
1 tablespoon lemon juice
1 (7-3/4-oz.) can salmon, drained,
   flaked
Potato chips or corn chips for dipping

Peel cucumber; coarsely grate or finely chop. Sprinkle with salt. Let stand at least 1 hour. Drain; press out excess liquid with back of spoon. In a medium bowl, combine drained cucumber, sour cream, mayonnaise, pepper, seasoned salt, dill weed and lemon juice. Add salmon; toss to distribute. Refrigerate until served. Serve with potato chips or corn chips for dipping. Makes about 2-3/4 cups.

Use very ripe avocados to make dips. Use less ripe avocados for slicing and garnishing.

Liverwurst Dip

So quick to make it is ideal for unexpected guests.

1/2 lb. liverwurst
1 cup dairy sour cream
1 (9/16-oz.) pkg. dry green onion
  dip mix

1 tablespoon steak sauce
3 or 4 drops hot pepper sauce
Rye crackers or party rye bread

In a medium bowl, combine liverwurst and sour cream, mashing liverwurst with a fork. Stir in onion dip mix, steak sauce and hot pepper sauce. Serve with rye crackers or party rye bread. Makes 2 cups.

Creamy Crab Dip

Delightfully rich and creamy.

1/2 cup dairy sour cream
1/2 cup mayonnaise
1 (3-oz.) pkg. cream cheese,
  room temperature
1 teaspoon Worcestershire sauce
1 garlic clove, crushed

1/4 teaspoon seasoned salt
1 tablespoon lemon juice
3 or 4 drops hot pepper sauce
1 (6-oz.) can crabmeat, drained, flaked
Potato chips or corn chips for dipping

In a medium bowl, combine sour cream, mayonnaise, cream cheese, Worcestershire sauce, garlic, seasoned salt, lemon juice and hot pepper sauce until blended. Stir in crabmeat. Refrigerate 3 to 4 hours before serving to blend flavors. Serve cold with potato chips or corn chips for dipping. Makes about 2 cups.

Party-Style Tostadas

Have taco sauce ready for guests who like hot foods.

1 lb. lean ground beef
1 (1-1/4-oz.) pkg. taco seasoning mix
3/4 cup water
1 (17-oz.) can refried beans
2 cups grated Cheddar cheese (8 oz.)

1 tomato, chopped
Guacamole, page 118
1/2 cup dairy sour cream
1/4 cup chopped green onions
Corn chips or tortilla chips for dipping

In a large skillet, brown beef, stirring with a fork to crumble. Pour off drippings. Stir in taco seasoning mix and water; simmer about 10 minutes. Preheat oven to 350°F (175°C). Spread meat mixture over bottom of a 9-inch square baking pan or 9-inch pie pan. Spoon beans evenly over top. Sprinkle evenly with cheese. Bake 10 to 12 minutes in preheated oven or until bubbly. Arrange chopped tomato, Guacamole, sour cream and onions over top. Serve immediately with corn chips or tortilla chips for dippers. Makes 10 to 15 appetizer servings.

Farm-Style Chili con Queso

Garden-fresh flavors make this dip extra special.

2 slices bacon, chopped
1 small onion, finely chopped
1 medium tomato, peeled, seeded, chopped
1/2 cup finely chopped celery
1 (7-oz.) can green chili salsa

1/4 teaspoon salt
2 cups grated Monterey Jack cheese
  (8 oz.)
Tortilla chips for dipping

In a medium skillet, cook bacon until most of fat is removed. Add onion, tomato and celery. Stirring occasionally, cook over medium heat until onion is tender. Stir in salsa and salt. Over low heat, stir in cheese until melted; do not boil. Pour into a small fondue pot or small bowl on a hot tray. Serve with tortilla chips for dipping. Makes 2-1/2 cups.

Hot Bean Dip

For variety, stir in three tablespoons chopped canned green chilies.

1 (16-oz.) can refried beans
1 (1-1/4-oz.) pkg. taco seasoning mix
3 green onions, finely chopped

1/2 cup dairy sour cream
1 cup grated sharp Cheddar cheese (4 oz.)
Corn chips for dipping

In a medium saucepan, combine beans, taco seasoning mix, onions, sour cream and cheese. Stir occasionally over low heat until cheese melts. Serve warm in fondue pot or medium bowl on a hot tray. Serve with corn chips for dipping. Makes 2-1/3 cups.

How to Make Farm-Style Chili con Queso

1/Add cheese to hot vegetable mixture; stir over low heat until cheese melts. Do not boil.

2/Keep mixture hot in heat-proof pot or bowl. Serve with corn chips or tortilla chips.

Refried Bean Dip

Serve this easy-to-prepare warm dip any season of the year.

1 (8-oz.) can refried beans
1 cup grated sharp Cheddar cheese (4 oz.)
1/2 teaspoon chili powder
1 teaspoon minced dried onion

1/8 teaspoon garlic salt
2 to 3 drops hot pepper sauce
Tortilla chips for dipping

In a small saucepan, combine beans, cheese, chili powder, onion, garlic salt and hot pepper sauce. Stir over low heat until cheese is melted; do not boil. Spoon into a small fondue pot or small bowl on a hot tray. Serve warm with tortilla chips for dipping. Makes about 1-1/4 cups.

North-of-the-Border Dip

This interesting blend of flavors is similar to an empanada filling.

1/2 lb. lean ground beef
1 small onion, chopped
1/2 teaspoon salt
1 garlic clove, minced
2 tomatoes, chopped
1 (6-oz.) can tomato paste

1 fresh or canned green chili pepper,
  seeded, chopped
1/4 cup chopped raisins
1/4 cup chopped toasted almonds
Corn chips for dipping

In a medium skillet, cook beef and onion until beef is browned. Stir with a fork or spoon to crumble meat. Remove drippings. Stir in salt, garlic, tomatoes, tomato paste, chili pepper and raisins. Stirring occasionally, cook over low heat about 10 minutes. Stir in almonds. Serve hot with corn chips for dipping. Makes 2-1/2 cups.

Moroccan Dip

Garbanzo beans provide an unusual dip for vegetables.

1 (15-oz.) can garbanzo beans, drained
2 tablespoons vegetable oil
1 tablespoon lemon juice
2 tablespoons chopped onion
1/2 teaspoon salt
1 teaspoon Worcestershire sauce

2 tablespoons sesame seeds
2 tablespoons chopped parsley
1 jicama, cut in sticks
1 carrot, cut in sticks
1/4 lb. broccoli, cut in flowerets

In blender, combine beans, oil, lemon juice and onion. Process until smooth. Add salt, Worcestershire sauce and sesame seeds. Process briefly. Spoon into a small serving dish; sprinkle with parsley. Serve with jicama sticks, carrot sticks and broccoli flowerets. Makes 1-1/2 cups.

Deviled Egg Dip

It tastes like deviled eggs in dip form.

1/4 cup mayonnaise
1 (3-oz.) pkg. cream cheese,
  room temperature
1 tablespoon milk
1 teaspoon prepared mustard
1/4 teaspoon salt

1/8 teaspoon pepper
1/4 teaspoon prepared horseradish
1 teaspoon chopped chives
4 hard-cooked eggs, finely chopped
Variety of crackers or raw vegetables

In a medium bowl, beat mayonnaise, cream cheese and milk until smooth. Stir in mustard, salt, pepper, horseradish, chives and hard-cooked eggs. Spoon into a small serving dish. Serve with a variety of crackers or raw vegetables. Makes 1-1/2 cups.

Tapenade

Try this traditional Mediterranean dip with chunks of French bread.

1 (2-oz.) can flat anchovy fillets,
  drained
1 (2-1/4-oz.) can sliced ripe olives,
  drained
1/4 cup drained capers
2 tablespoons lemon juice

1 tablespoon Dijon-style mustard
1/8 teaspoon pepper
1/3 cup olive oil or vegetable oil
French bread, cut in thick slices, or
  raw vegetable dippers

Coarsely chop anchovies. In blender, combine chopped anchovies, olives, capers, lemon juice, mustard and pepper. Process until pureed. On low speed, gradually add oil, blending to make a thick paste. Serve with thick slices of French bread or raw vegetable dippers. Makes 1 cup.

Variation

Tuna Tapenade: Add 1 tablespoon sherry wine and 1 (6-oz.) can tuna, drained. Reduce oil to 1 tablespoon. Omit mustard.

Bagna Cauda

This is a favorite dip made in many Italian kitchens.

1/2 cup butter or margarine
1/3 cup olive oil or vegetable oil
2 cloves garlic, crushed
1 (2-oz.) can flat anchovy fillets,
  drained, chopped

2 tablespoons minced parsley
Celery sticks, green pepper strips,
  tomato wedges and
  zucchini slices for dipping

In a small saucepan, heat butter or margarine and oil. Add garlic and anchovies. Bring to a simmer over medium heat; do not boil. Pour into a small fondue pot or small bowl on a hot tray. Sprinkle with parsley. Serve hot with vegetables for dipping. Makes 1 cup.

Nibblers & Dippers

Set the stage for relaxed entertaining with fun foods and a casual atmosphere. A ready supply of Party Nibblers or Teriyaki Toasted Nuts gives the busy homemaker a headstart for successful impromptu gatherings. In minutes, dishes of these delicious snacks are placed around the room for convenient munching. Guests can relax with foods close at hand or move from place to place to sample other delectables, from Hot Pecans to Smoky Almonds. All are easily prepared in very little time with excellent results.

Before commercial potato chips were available, people made them at home. Now you can make your own, too. The process is fairly simple, requiring fresh potatoes, oil for deep-frying and salt to taste. Soak the potato slices in salted water to keep them from turning dark. After drying the potatoes in a 250°F (120°C) oven for 15 minutes, deep-fry them in a mini deep-fryer. This gives you less greasy potato chips that are evenly cooked. Automatic temperature controls on small electric deep-fryers keep the oil at about 375°F (190°C) while you're cooking. These small' cookers cost less to heat and use less oil than large deep-fryers. Most deep-fried appetizers require a 375°F (190°C) temperature. One exception is Noodle Chips which must be fried at 400°F (205°C). Pour the oil into an electric saucepan or frying pan that can be brought to that heat, or use a narrow, deep saucepan and a cooking thermometer. Use any cooking oil except strong-flavored olive oil. Butter, margarine and lard are not suitable because they smoke and burn at a low temperature.

Get some friends together and have a good time making Homemade Soft Pretzels, Sesame Crackers and Mini Bagels. These take a little more time than other snacks, but your results are guaranteed to be worth every minute spent in the kitchen. Whole-wheat enthusiasts will want to try Mini Bagels made with part or all whole-wheat flour. Whether you already enjoy making bread or this is your first attempt, you'll find these three basic steps easy to follow. First, make the dough, let it rise and shape it into small donuts. Second, carefully lower the shaped dough into simmering water where the bagels puff and cook. Next, bake them 15 minutes at 400°F (205°C) until lightly browned. Homemade bagels are easy to make, easy on the budget and contain no preservatives.

Noodle Chips   Photo on page 129.

Use corkscrew, bow-shaped or butterfly noodles to make these chips.

1 (8-oz.) pkg. corkscrew egg noodles   **Garlic salt or seasoned salt**
Oil for deep-frying

Cook noodles in boiling water according to package directions; drain. Immediately run cold water over noodles; drain again. Pat noodles with paper towels, removing as much moisture as possible. Pour oil 2 inches deep into a large skillet or large heavy saucepan. Heat to 400°F (205°C). At this temperature a 1-inch cube of bread will turn golden brown in about 20 seconds. Lower 6 or 7 cooked, drained noodles into hot fat. Fry until golden brown; drain on paper towels. Sprinkle with garlic salt or seasoned salt. Use as snacks or dip chips. Makes 6 to 7 cups.

Homemade Tortilla Chips

Fresh, crispy and easy on the budget.

12 corn tortillas   **Salt, if desired**
Oil for deep-frying

Cut each tortilla into 8 to 10 wedges. Pour oil for deep-frying 3 inches deep into an electric deep-fryer or to level suggested by manufacturer. Or pour oil 2 inches deep into a large skillet or large heavy saucepan. Heat oil to 375°F (190°C). At this temperature a 1-inch cube of bread will turn golden brown in 40 seconds. Carefully lower 4 or 5 tortilla wedges at a time into hot oil. Fry until crisp, turning once with tongs. Drain on paper towels; sprinkle with salt, if desired. Makes 96 to 120 chips.

Potato Chips

Oven drying the raw potato slices makes them more crisp.

2 medium potatoes   **Salt to taste**
Oil for deep-frying

Peel potatoes. Use a vegetable peeler or slicer on a hand grater or food processor to cut potatoes into very thin slices, less than 1/16 inch thick. In a medium bowl, soak potato slices in cold water to cover 30 minutes, changing water once. Preheat oven to 250°F (120°C). Drain potatoes; pat dry with paper towels. Place wire rack on a baking sheet. Arrange potato slices in single layer on rack. Bake 15 to 20 minutes in preheated oven or until completely dry. Remove from oven. Pour oil for deep-frying 3 inches deep into an electric deep-fryer or to level suggested by manufacturer. Or pour oil 2 inches deep into a large skillet or large heavy saucepan. Heat oil to 375°F (190°C). At this temperature, a 1-inch cube of bread will turn golden brown in 40 seconds. Fry 5 or 6 dry potato slices at a time in hot oil 2 to 2-1/2 minutes or until crisp and golden. Use a slotted spoon to remove cooked slices from hot oil; drain on paper towels. Sprinkle hot potato slices with salt to taste. Makes 60 to 80 chips.

Mini Bagels

Serve these glazed, seed studded bagels with cream cheese and lox or your favorite spread.

1 envelope active dry yeast
1/4 cup warm water (110°F, 45°C)
1/4 cup butter or margarine,
  room temperature
1 tablespoon sugar
1 teaspoon salt
1 cup water

1 egg, separated
3-3/4 to 4 cups all-purpose flour
2 quarts water
2 tablespoons sugar
1 tablespoon water
Poppy seeds or sesame seeds, if desired

In a large bowl, stir yeast into 1/4 cup warm water until dissolved. Add butter or margarine, 1 tablespoon sugar, salt, 1 cup water, egg white and 1-1/2 cups flour. Beat with electric mixer about 3 minutes until smooth. Add enough of the remaining flour to make a soft dough. Turn out on a lightly floured board. Knead about 5 minutes or until smooth and elastic. Clean and lightly grease bowl. Place dough in bowl, turning to grease all sides. Cover and let rise in a warm place until doubled in bulk, about 1 hour. Punch down; knead 1 to 2 minutes. Divide into 4 pieces; divide each piece into 10 equal pieces. With palms of your hands, roll each piece into a 6-inch rope. Shape each rope into a ring with ends overlapping slightly. Pinch ends together to seal. Let rest about 15 minutes until they begin to rise. In a 4-quart pot or Dutch oven, heat 2 quarts water and 2 tablespoons sugar to a simmer; do not boil. Grease a large baking sheet; set aside. Use a slotted spoon to lower bagels 3 or 4 at a time into simmering water. Cook 1 minute on each side. Carefully remove bagels from hot water; drain briefly on paper towels. Arrange on prepared baking sheet. Preheat oven to 400°F (205°C). In a small bowl, beat egg yolk and 1 tablespoon water. Brush bagels with egg yolk mixture. Sprinkle with poppy seeds or sesame seeds, if desired. Bake about 15 minutes in preheated oven until lightly browned. Makes forty 2-inch bagels.

Variation
Substitute whole-wheat flour for all-purpose flour.

Pita Bread

Cut the bread into wedges for dippers or cut them in half and use as pocket breads.

1 envelope active dry yeast
1 teaspoon sugar
1/4 cup warm water (110°F, 45°C)
4 cups all-purpose flour

1 teaspoon salt
2 tablespoons vegetable oil
1-1/2 cups warm water (110°F, 45°C)

In a small bowl, dissolve yeast and sugar in 1/4 cup warm water; set aside about 5 minutes until foamy. In a large bowl, combine flour and salt. Make a well in center; add yeast mixture, oil and 1-1/2 cups warm water. Gradually mix into flour until evenly distributed. Shape dough into a ball. Turn out on a lightly floured board. Knead 7 to 8 minutes or until smooth, adding more flour if necessary to make a fairly stiff dough. Clean and grease bowl. Place kneaded dough in greased bowl, turning to grease all sides. Cover and let rise in a warm place until doubled in bulk, about 1-1/4 hours. Grease several large baking sheets; set aside. Punch down dough; knead 1 to 2 minutes. Divide dough into 12 equal pieces. Use a rolling pin to roll each piece to a 6-inch circle. Arrange on prepared baking sheets. Cover and let rise in a warm place until doubled, about 40 minutes. Preheat oven to 500°F (260°C). Place oven rack in center of oven. Bake 1 pan at a time on rack, 5 to 7 minutes until puffed and lightly browned. Makes 12 pita breads.

How to Make Mini Bagels

1/Shape small pieces of dough into 6-inch ropes. Overlap ends to make a circle.

2/Brush drained bagels with egg yolk mixture. Sprinkle with poppy seeds or sesame seeds. Bake 15 minutes.

Crepe Chips

Use these delicately thin chips with light dips or for snacking by themselves.

4 cooked All-Purpose Crepes, page 86
1 tablespoon butter or margarine, melted
Seasoned salt
Garlic salt

Dried dill weed, crushed
Mexican seasoning
Grated Parmesan cheese

Preheat oven to 325°F (165°C). Brush crepes with butter or margarine. Season by sprinkling with one or more of the remaining ingredients. Cut each crepe into quarters. Cut each quarter into 3 or 4 wedges. Arrange on an ungreased baking sheet, seasoned-side up. Bake 6 to 9 minutes in preheated oven until crisp. Makes 48 to 64 chips.

Homemade Soft Pretzels

Eat them plain or spread butter and mustard over them.

3-1/2 to 3-3/4 cups all-purpose flour
1 envelope active dry yeast
1-1/4 cups milk
1/2 cup butter or margarine
1 tablespoon sugar

1/2 teaspoon salt
1 egg, separated
1 tablespoon water
Coarse salt or sesame seeds

In a large bowl, combine 1-1/2 cups flour and yeast. Make a well in center; set aside. In a small saucepan, combine milk, butter or margarine, sugar and salt. Stir constantly over low heat until butter or margarine melts; cool slightly. Pour warm milk mixture and unbeaten egg white into well in flour mixture. Beat about 3 minutes with electric mixer. Stir in enough of the remaining flour to make a soft dough. Turn out on a lightly floured board; knead about 5 minutes or until dough is smooth and elastic. Clean and grease bowl. Place kneaded dough in greased bowl, turning to grease all sides. Cover and let rise in warm place until doubled in bulk, about 1 hour. Punch down; let rest 10 minutes. Divide into 20 equal pieces. With palms of your hands, roll each piece into a 16-inch rope. Shape each rope into a pretzel by laying the rope in a U-shape with ends pointing away from you. Wrap rope ends around each other at least once. Keeping rope ends separated, lift ends and twisted portion toward you. Lay rope ends on top of closed end of U. Pinch ends into closed portion to seal. Let rest on board about 15 minutes until pretzels begin to rise. Pour water 4 inches deep into a 4-quart pot or Dutch oven. Bring to a simmer over medium heat; do not boil. Grease a large baking sheet; set aside. Use a slotted spoon to lower pretzels one or two at a time into simmering water. Cook 30 seconds on each side, turning once. Use slotted spoon to remove pretzels from hot water; drain briefly on paper towels. Preheat oven to 400°F (205°C). Arrange drained pretzels on prepared baking sheet. In a small bowl, beat egg yolk and 1 tablespoon water. Brush evenly over pretzels. Sprinkle with coarse salt or sesame seeds. Bake about 15 minutes in preheated oven until lightly browned. Makes 20 pretzels.

Nachos

Slighty messy, but fun to eat.

4 cups corn chips or tortilla chips
3 cups shredded Cheddar cheese (12 oz.)

1/4 cup chopped green chilies, drained

Preheat oven to 400°F (205°C). Arrange corn chips or tortilla chips on a 12-inch pizza pan, overlapping slightly. Sprinkle evenly with Cheddar cheese. Bake 5 to 7 minutes in preheated oven until cheese melts. Sprinkle evenly with chilies. Serve immediately, picking up cheese-coated chips with your fingers. Makes 4 to 6 servings.

Clockwise from upper right, Teriyaki Toasted Nuts, page 130; Noodle Chips, page 125 in basket; Curried Sunflower Seeds, page 131.

Party Nibblers

Vary this mix with your favorite nuts or prepared dry cereal.

1 cup thin pretzel sticks
1 cup shelled peanuts
1-1/2 cups round oat cereal
1 cup chow mein noodles
1-1/2 cups miniature shredded wheat or
   rice cereal squares

1/3 cup butter or margarine
1 tablespoon Worcestershire sauce
1/2 teaspoon garlic salt
1/2 teaspoon chili powder
1/2 teaspoon celery salt

In a large bowl, mix pretzel sticks, peanuts, oat cereal, chow mein noodles and shredded wheat or rice squares; set aside. Preheat oven to 300°F (150°C). In a small saucepan, melt butter or margarine; stir in Worcestershire sauce, garlic salt, chili powder and celery salt. Pour over cereal mixture. Stir until evenly distributed. Spread coated cereal mixture on an ungreased baking sheet with raised sides. Bake 15 to 20 minutes in preheated oven, stirring once. Makes about 6 cups.

Teriyaki Toasted Nuts   Photo on page 129.

Use unsalted nuts if you prefer a less salty snack.

2 cups mixed nuts
2 tablespoons butter or margarine
1 tablespoon soy sauce

1/2 teaspoon ground ginger
1/4 teaspoon garlic salt
1 teaspoon lemon juice

Preheat oven to 325°F (165°C). Spread nuts on a large ungreased baking sheet with raised sides. Roast nuts 5 to 10 minutes until lightly browned. In a small skillet, melt butter or margarine. Stir in soy sauce, ginger, garlic salt and lemon juice; brush over toasted nuts. Roast 5 minutes longer until golden brown. Makes 2 cups.

Hot Pecans

These are excellent nibblers for any occasion.

2 cups pecan halves
3 tablespoons butter or margarine, melted
1 teaspoon chili powder
1/8 teaspoon cayenne pepper

1 garlic clove, crushed
1/4 teaspoon salt
1/4 teaspoon ground coriander

Preheat oven to 350°F (175°C). Spread pecans over bottom of a large baking sheet with raised sides. Bake 7 minutes until heated through. In a small bowl, combine butter or margarine, chili powder, cayenne pepper, garlic, salt and coriander. Stir pecans; brush with sauce. Bake 5 minutes longer. Serve warm or cool. Makes 2 cups.

Smoky Almonds

The flavor is similar to barbecued foods.

2 cups whole blanched almonds
2 tablespoons butter or margarine, melted
1/4 teaspoon seasoned salt

1/4 teaspoon liquid smoke seasoning
1/8 teaspoon garlic salt

Preheat oven to 350°F (175°C). Spread almonds over bottom of a large baking sheet with raised sides. Bake 8 to 10 minutes until light golden brown. In a small bowl, combine butter or margarine, seasoned salt, liquid smoke and garlic salt. Stir almonds; brush with sauce. Bake 5 minutes longer. Serve warm or cool. Makes 2 cups.

Curried Sunflower Seeds   Photo on page 129.

Keep a bag of these in the freezer to serve to unexpected guests.

1 teaspoon curry powder
1/2 teaspoon seasoned salt

1/8 teaspoon garlic salt
1 cup sunflower seeds

Preheat oven to 325°F (165°C). In a small bowl, combine curry powder, seasoned salt, garlic salt and sunflower seeds. Spread evenly on an ungreased baking sheet. Toast 10 to 15 minutes in preheated oven until golden brown. Makes 1 cup.

Cheese Cookies

Allow two to three minutes additional baking time when you chill the dough.

3/4 cup butter or margarine,
  room temperature
1/4 cup grated Parmesan cheese (1 oz.)
1-1/2 cups shredded sharp Cheddar cheese
  (6 oz.)

1/2 teaspoon paprika
1 teaspoon Worcestershire sauce
1/2 teaspoon dry mustard
1/2 teaspoon salt
1-1/2 cups all-purpose flour

Preheat oven to 350°F (175°C). In a large bowl, beat butter or margarine, Parmesan cheese and Cheddar cheese until smooth. Stir in paprika, Worcestershire sauce, mustard, salt and flour until thoroughly blended. Spoon into a cookie press; attach ribbon point. Press through point onto 2 ungreased baking sheets making 2-inch ribbon cookies. Or divide dough in half; shape each half into a 6" x 1-1/2 " roll. Refrigerate rolls at least 1 hour. Cut each into 25 slices. Arrange slices 1/2 inch apart on ungreased baking sheets. Bake 10 to 12 minutes in preheated oven until golden brown. Serve warm. Makes about 50 cookies.

Sesame Crackers

Wrap these thin crackers airtight and keep them in your freezer as long as six months.

1 cup whole-wheat flour	1/2 teaspoon salt
1 cup all-purpose flour	1/4 cup vegetable oil
1/4 cup sesame seeds	1/2 cup water

In a medium bowl, combine whole-wheat flour and all-purpose flour, sesame seeds and salt. Make a well in center; pour oil and water into well. Stir into flour mixture until blended. Preheat oven to 350°F (175°C). Shape dough into a ball; roll out 1/8 inch thick on a lightly floured board. Cut into 2" x 1" strips. Arrange on an ungreased baking sheet. Bake 15 to 20 minutes in preheated oven until golden brown. Makes 75 to 85 crackers.

Green Onion & Cheese Crackers

Eat these crunchy nibblers warm or cool, by themselves or served with a ham spread.

1/2 cup butter or margarine, room temperature	1 (9/16-oz.) pkg. dry green onion dip mix
2 cups shredded Cheddar cheese (8 oz.)	1-1/4 cups all-purpose flour

In a large bowl, beat butter or margarine and Cheddar cheese until smooth. Stir in dip mix and flour. Divide dough in half; shape into a two 5-inch rolls. Wrap airtight and refrigerate 3 to 4 hours. Preheat oven to 375°F (190°C). Grease a large baking sheet. Cut rolls into 1/4-inch slices. Bake on prepared baking sheet 10 to 12 minutes in preheated oven until browned around edges. Makes about 40 crackers.

Garlic Cheese Thins

Serve these as a snack or as an accompaniment to a salad.

2 (6-inch) sourdough rolls	1 garlic clove, crushed
1/2 cup butter or margarine	1/2 cup grated Parmesan cheese (2 oz.)

Cut rolls into very thin slices. Arrange in a single layer on an ungreased baking sheet; set aside. Preheat oven to 300°F (150°C). In a small saucepan, melt butter or margarine. Stir in garlic until tender, about 2 minutes. Stir in cheese. Use a pastry brush to spread over bread slices. Bake about 15 minutes in preheated oven until crisp. Makes 60 to 65 slices.

How to Make Sesame Crackers

1/Use the back of spoon to push flour mixture to side of bowl to make well.

2/Use a pastry cutter or a sharp knife to cut dough into 2" x 1" strips.

Cheese Sticks

Good soups are made even better when served with these tasty sticks.

**1/4 cup butter or margarine,
  room temperature**
**1 cup shredded sharp Cheddar cheese
  (4 oz.)**
2 tablespoons grated Parmesan cheese

1 teaspoon Worcestershire sauce
1/4 teaspoon chili powder
1/4 teaspoon celery salt
1/2 cup all-purpose flour

In a small bowl, combine butter or margarine, Cheddar cheese, Parmesan cheese, Worcestershire sauce, chili powder and celery salt, beating until smooth. Stir in flour until blended. Wrap dough airtight in foil or plastic wrap. Refrigerate at least 1 hour. Preheat oven to 375°F (190°C). Pinch off walnut-size pieces of chilled dough. Roll each piece between your palms to make 4-inch pencil-like ropes, about 1/4 inch thick. Arrange on an ungreased baking sheet. Bake 8 to 10 minutes in pre-heated oven until golden brown. Makes about 30 sticks.

Party Sandwiches

Party sandwiches are appetizer show-offs. Cut them into squares, triangles, fingers and ribbons or leave them *au naturel.* For more unusual designs, use hors d'oeuvre or cookie cutters with fluted or scalloped edges. Some are shaped like hearts, flowers, animals or fruits. Party sandwiches are an inexpensive way to dress up a small tray of assorted appetizers for three or four people. Or they can provide the bulk of refreshment for 100 people. What could be more thrifty than using two cups of meat, poultry, fish or cheese filling for 45 to 50 party sandwiches?

Make sandwiches ahead for a large gathering such as a wedding reception, bridal or baby shower, graduation celebration or golden wedding anniversary. Ribbon, checkerboard, pinwheel and double sandwiches may be made and stored in the refrigerator one to three days. Or store in the freezer up to three months if the filling ingredients can be frozen. See *Preparing & Storing Appetizers*, page 7.

Make sandwiches from at least two different breads for eye and appetite appeal. Bakery breads come in a wide variety of types and flavors. You may prefer Molasses Round Bread baked in emptied 16-ounce metal cans. It is the ideal size for sandwiches.

Decorative sandwiches pictured on the following pages are made with lengthwise sliced bread. Most bakeries will do the slicing for you but require at least one-day's notice. Cut your own slices from an unsliced loaf if your bakery does not provide this service. Sandwich bread has uniform shape with squared ends. This means less waste than you'd have with standard loaves. Partially freeze the loaf before using your sharpest knife to cut off crusts one side at a time. Because they help hold the loaf firm, cut off ends last. With a sawing motion, cut five to seven 1/2-inch horizontal slices. To make two-colored ribbon or checkerboard sandwiches, you'll need two loaves of bread the same size—one light and one dark.

Open-face sandwiches are easily made from standard bread slices or thinly sliced sandwich bread. Prepare the bread, filling and garnishes separately and keep each covered in the refrigerator. Assemble the sandwiches an hour or two before serving. This is one of those times it would be wise to have help with preparation.

Make small roll-ups from thinly sliced standard loaf bread or sandwich bread. To make neat rolls, remove the crusts and lightly press each slice of bread with a rolling pin.

Garnishes for Party Sandwiches

Mix and match according to taste, color and texture of filling and bread:

Anchovies, flat or rolled
Beets, pickled, sliced
Capers
Carrot, sliced
Celery leaves
Cherry tomatoes, sliced
Chives or green onion, chopped
Cilantro leaves
Cucumber, sliced
Curly endive leaves
Dill weed, fresh
Eggs, hard-cooked, sliced or diced

Mushrooms, sliced
Nuts, chopped
Olives, green or ripe, sliced
Parsley, chopped
Pepper, red or green, sliced
Pickles, chopped or sliced
Pimiento, chopped or sliced
Radishes, sliced
Tarragon leaves, fresh
Water chestnuts, sliced
Watercress

Pinwheel Sandwiches

1/Trim crusts from unsliced sandwich bread. Cut into five to seven 1/2-inch horizontal slices. Spread with butter or margarine, then filling. Beginning at the narrow end, roll up tightly jelly-roll fashion.

2/Wrap tightly in plastic wrap or foil and store rolled sandiches in refrigerator or freezer at least 24 hours. Remove wrap. Use a non-serrated knife to cut each roll into 8 to 12 crosswise slices. Cover and refrigerate until served.

Mosaic Sandwiches

1/Trim crusts from 1 loaf each of light and dark sandwich bread. Cut each loaf into 5 to 7 horizontal slices. Use cookie cutters to cut into desired shapes. Same colors may be sandwiched with filling between them or use one of each color.

2/Use hors d'oeuvre cutters to cut centers from 1/2 of the light and 1/2 of the dark bread. Spread filling on uncut pieces; top with outer rings of cut pieces. Matching cut-outs, insert light centers into dark bread and dark centers into light bread. Cover and refrigerate until served.

Sandwich Spreads

Plan on 1/2 cup plain or flavored spread for 45 to 50 open-face sandwiches.

Mustard: Combine 1 tablespoon prepared mustard and 1/2 cup butter or margarine.

Chive: Combine 1 tablespoon minced chives and 1/2 cup butter or margarine.

Herb: Combine 1/4 teaspoon crushed dried rosemary leaves, 1/4 teaspoon crushed dried basil leaves, 1/8 teaspoon crushed dried thyme leaves and 1/2 cup butter or margarine.

Dill: Combine 1 teaspoon dried dill weed and 1/2 cup butter or margarine.

Ribbon Sandwiches

1/Trim crusts from 1 loaf each of light and dark sandwich bread. Cut each into 5 to 7 horizontal slices. Spread butter or margarine and filling on 2 white slices and 1 dark slice. Stack, alternating color of bread. Top with an unspread slice. Repeat with remaining slices, alternating colors.

2/Wrap in foil or plastic wrap. Refrigerate or freeze 2 to 4 hours or several days. Partially thaw before cutting each stack into 15 to 20 crosswise slices. Cut each slice in half for smaller sandwiches. Cover and refrigerate until served.

Italian: Combine 1/2 teaspoon crushed dried oregano leaves, 1/2 teaspoon crushed dried basil leaves, 1/2 teaspoon garlic salt and 1/2 cup butter or margarine.

Anchovy: Combine 2 teaspoons anchovy paste, 1/2 teaspoon lemon juice and 1/2 cup mayonnaise.

Rémoulade: Combine 1 tablespoon chopped capers, 1 tablespoon minced chives, 1 teaspoon dried oregano leaves and 1/2 cup mayonnaise.

Cheese: Combine 1/4 cup grated Parmesan cheese or 2 tablespoons crumbled Roquefort cheese, 1 teaspoon chopped parsley and 1/2 cup mayonnaise or dairy sour cream.

Watercress: Combine 1/4 cup minced watercress leaves, 1 tablespoon minced chives and 1/2 cup dairy sour cream.

Parsley & Pimiento: Combine 2 tablespoons chopped parsley, 2 tablespoons chopped pimiento and 1/2 cup butter or margarine.

Checkerboard Sandwiches

1/Prepare bread and assemble with filling as for Ribbon Sandwiches, using 4 layers; refrigerate or freeze. Cut thoroughly chilled loaves into slices. Stack 4 slices, alternating colors of bread with butter or margarine spread between layers. Press slices together gently but firmly.

2/Wrap each stack individually in foil or plastic wrap. Refrigerate or freeze 2 to 4 hours or several days. Partially thaw frozen sandwiches. Cut cold sandwich stacks into four or five 1/2- to 3/4-inch slices. Cut in half for smaller sandwiches. Cover and refrigerate until served.

Ham Filling

Use a food grinder or a food processor to grind the ham.

2 cups ground cooked ham
1/3 cup mayonnaise

1 teaspoon prepared mustard
1 tablespoon drained sweet pickle relish

In a small bowl, combine ham, mayonnaise, mustard and relish. Makes 1-1/2 cups.

Variations

Add one or more of the following:

1 chopped hard-cooked egg

1/4 cup shredded Cheddar cheese (1-oz.)

1 green onion, finely chopped

2 tablespoons minced green pepper

Cream Cheese Filling

For a mild flavor, use only the cheese and milk, or add one or more of the variations.

**1 (3-oz.) pkg. cream cheese,
   room temperature**

1 tablespoon milk

In a small bowl, mix cream cheese and milk until smooth. Makes 1/3 cup.

Variations

Add one or more of the following:

1 tablespoon minced chives and 1 tablespoon minced pimiento.

2 tablespoons chopped walnuts or pecans

2 tablespoons chopped dates or raisins

1/4 cup drained, chopped ripe or stuffed green olives

2 tablespoons crumbled cooked bacon

1 tablespoon finely chopped chutney

2 tablespoons finely chopped watercress leaves

2 tablespoons crumbled blue cheese

Egg Filling

Egg fillings stretch your budget when making party sandwiches.

4 hard-cooked eggs, chopped
1/4 cup mayonnaise
1/2 teaspoon prepared mustard

1/4 teaspoon salt
1/8 teaspoon pepper

In a small bowl, combine eggs, mayonnaise, mustard, salt and pepper. Makes about 1 cup.

Variations

Add one or more of the following:

2 slices crisp-cooked bacon, crumbled

1/4 cup finely chopped cooked ham and 1 teaspoon drained sweet pickle relish

1/2 teaspoon dried dill weed, crushed, and 1 teaspoon freshly minced chives

1/4 cup drained, finely chopped ripe olives

Immerse hot hard-cooked eggs in cold water until cool, then remove shells. Use immediately or refrigerate in a plastic bag or covered dish. Use within several hours.

Chicken or Turkey Filling

Fill puffs or fancy sandwiches with this mixture. Serve them at receptions or open houses.

2 cups ground cooked chicken or ground cooked turkey	1/3 cup mayonnaise
1/4 cup finely chopped celery	1/8 teaspoon salt
	Pinch pepper

In a small bowl, combine chicken, celery, mayonnaise, salt and pepper. Makes about 1-1/2 cups.

Variations

Add one or more of the following:

1/4 cup chopped toasted almonds or pecans

1 tablespoon drained sweet pickle relish and 1/2 teaspoon dried minced onion

1 hard-cooked egg, chopped, and 1/2 teaspoon prepared mustard

1/4 cup drained, crushed pineapple and 1 tablespoon finely chopped Macadamia nuts

1/4 cup chopped water chestnuts and 1 teaspoon soy sauce

Tuna Filling

Tuna is a favorite of any age group.

1 (6-1/2-oz.) can tuna, drained, flaked	1/4 cup minced celery
1/3 cup mayonnaise	1 tablespoon finely chopped sweet pickle

In a small bowl, combine tuna, mayonnaise, celery and pickle. Makes about 1-1/4 cups.

Variations

Add one or more of the following:

1 hard-cooked egg, chopped, and 1 teaspoon minced pimiento

1/2 ripe avocado, chopped, and 1 teaspoon lemon juice

1 tablespoon chopped capers

Corned Beef Filling

Spoon this interesting filling into Petite Toast Cups, page 78, or spread on party rye.

2 cups finely chopped, cooked corned beef	2 tablespoons finely chopped dill pickle
1 tablespoon prepared mustard	1/2 cup mayonnaise
2 teaspoon prepared horseradish	

In a medium bowl, combine all ingredients. Makes about 2-1/4 cups.

Medley of Party Sandwiches with cream cheese piping

Elegant Crab Filling

This may be a little extravagant, but it's a nice filling for party sandwiches.

2 (3-oz.) pkgs. cream cheese,
  room temperature
2 tablespoons dry white wine
1 teaspoon lemon juice
1/2 teaspoon seasoned salt
1 teaspoon grated onion

1/8 teaspoon dried dill weed
1 (6-oz.) can crabmeat or
  1 (6-oz.) pkg. frozen crabmeat
Crackers or Melba toast rounds
Fresh dill for garnish, if desired

In a small bowl, beat cream cheese, wine, lemon juice, seasoned salt, onion and dill weed; set aside. Drain and flake canned crabmeat or thaw, drain and flake frozen crabmeat. Stir flaked crabmeat into cheese mixture. Refrigerate 3 to 4 hours. Spread on crackers or Melba toast. Garnish with fresh dill if desired. Makes 1 cup.

Superb Peanut Butter Spread

Peanut butter combinations are especially good spread on fruit breads.

3/4 cup peanut butter
1/4 cup mayonnaise
1 tablespoon orange marmalade or
  apricot jam

4 slices crisp-cooked bacon, crumbled
Banana nut bread or date nut bread,
  thinly sliced

In a small bowl, combine peanut butter, mayonnaise and marmalade or jam. Stir in bacon. Spread on slices of banana-nut bread or date-nut bread. Makes about 1 cup.

Green Mayonnaise

This is equally delicious on party sandwiches or as a topping for fish molds.

1 cup mayonnaise
2 tablespoons chopped watercress
1 tablespoon chopped chives

1/4 teaspoon dried dill weed
1/2 teaspoon dried tarragon leaves
1/4 teaspoon seasoned salt

In blender or food processor, combine mayonnaise, watercress, chives, dill weed, tarragon and seasoned salt. Process until almost smooth. Makes about 1 cup.

Molasses Round Bread

Save empty 16-ounce cans. They're ideal for baking this rich brown bread.

1/4 cup butter or margarine
1/2 cup packed brown sugar
2 eggs
1 cup applesauce
1/4 cup molasses
1-1/4 cups all-purpose flour

1 cup whole-wheat flour
2 teaspoons baking powder
1 teaspoon baking soda
1/2 teaspoon salt
1/2 cup raisins

Preheat oven to 350°F (175°C). Thoroughly wash, dry, grease and flour 3 empty 16-ounce cans; set aside. In a large bowl, cream butter or margarine and sugar until smooth and fluffy. Beat in eggs. Stir in applesauce and molasses until thoroughly blended. In a medium bowl, combine all-purpose flour, whole-wheat flour, baking powder, baking soda and salt. Stir into creamed mixture until blended. Stir in raisins. Spoon batter evenly into 3 prepared cans. Bake 40 to 45 minutes in preheated oven until tops are golden brown. Cool in cans about 5 minutes; remove cans. Cool to room temperature on rack before slicing. Cut into thin slices. Spread half of slices with your choice of fillings. Top each with another slice; cut in half. Makes three 4-inch loaves.

Hawaiian Nut Bread

With this delicious bread, all you need is a mild-flavored spread.

2/3 cup sugar
1/3 cup vegetable shortening
2 eggs
1 cup mashed ripe bananas
   (about 2 medium)
1 (8-oz.) can crushed pineapple, drained

1/2 cup chopped Macadamia nuts or pecans
2 cups all-purpose flour
1 teaspoon baking powder
1/2 teaspoon baking soda
1/4 teaspoon salt
Butter or cream cheese, room temperature

Preheat oven to 350°F (175°C). Grease a 9'' x 5'' loaf pan. In a large bowl, cream sugar and shortening until fluffy; beat in eggs. Stir in mashed bananas, drained pineapple and nuts. In a medium bowl, combine flour, baking powder, baking soda and salt. Stir into banana mixture until smooth. Spoon into prepared pan. Bake 50 to 60 minutes in preheated oven. Remove from pan; cool on a rack. Wrap airtight in foil or plastic wrap; let stand overnight for easy slicing. To serve, cut into 1/4- to 1/2-inch slices. Spread with butter or cream cheese. Cut each slice in half, quarters or fingers. Makes 1 loaf or 50 to 80 appetizer servings.

For an impressive finishing touch on party sandwiches, drop by spoon or pipe from a pastry bag with a small star tip: mayonnaise, sour cream, yogurt, softened cream cheese or process cheese spread.

Miniature Reubens

Use left over corned beef or make thin slices from the canned variety.

24 slices cocktail rye bread
3 tablespoons Thousand Island dressing
24 small thin slices cooked corned beef

1 (8-oz.) can sauerkraut or
1 cup refrigerated sauerkraut, drained
3/4 cup shredded Swiss cheese (3 oz.)

Preheat broiler if necessary. Place oven rack 3 to 5 inches from heating element. Arrange single layer of bread on an ungreased baking sheet. Spread each with thin coating of dressing. Place 1 slice corned beef on each. Top evenly with sauerkraut. Sprinkle Swiss cheese evenly over sauerkraut. Broil until bubbly, 2 to 3 minutes. Serve hot. Makes 24 appetizer servings.

Swedish Open-Face Sandwiches

For special parties, this combination will be a winner.

3 hard-cooked eggs
1 (2-oz.) can flat anchovy fillets, drained
1/4 cup butter, room temperature
1 tablespoon Dijon-style mustard
1 tablespoon dried dill weed

1 tablespoon freshly minced parsley
1 tablespoon freshly minced chives
1/8 teaspoon pepper
24 slices party rye bread
Pimiento strips for garnish

Slice hard-cooked eggs; set aside. In a small bowl, use a fork to mash anchovies. Stir in butter until blended. Stir in mustard, dill weed, parsley, chives and pepper. Spread about 1 teaspoon anchovy mixture evenly over each bread slice. Top each with 1 egg slice and 1 small strip pimiento. Makes 24 open-face sandwiches.

Cutting Party Sandwiches

Use fancy cookie cutters or hors d'oeuvre cutters to make sandwiches which fit the theme of your party. Hearts and bells are especially pretty for wedding or anniversary parties; animal designs are appropriate for baby showers or children parties; stars and wreaths keep you in the spirit for holiday events. For a special effect, make fancy cut-out sandwiches by using a fluted, scalloped or round cookie cutter to cut 24 sandwich bases. Use an hors d'oeuvre cutter to cut out a decorative deign from the center of eight of the bases. Spread filling over each base with the center intact. Place a cut-out center or the bread from which it was cut on top of each filling.

Microwaved Appetizers

The microwave oven is the cook's best friend when it comes to preparing appetizers because it microwaves mini-morsels in a fraction of traditional cooking time. With today's emphasis on nutrition and small quick meals, these appetizers can be a perfect snack or dinner solution. When you plan the prelude to an elegant party or an impromptu neighborly get together, your microwave stands ready to make one of our favorite appetizers. Some of the following recipes take a little plan-ahead time for meat to marinate, but others can be made in minutes from food you have on hand.

When microwaving appetizers, remember to arrange larger or thicker foods on the outside edge of the dish; smaller ones in the center. The result will be more even cooking. Also, if your microwave doesn't have a carousel, it's a good idea to rotate the dish a quarter-turn during the cooking process to assure each morsel equal heat penetration. It doesn't matter whether you turn it clockwise or counter clockwise. If you can stir the ingredients, rotation is not necessary.

We've indicated the kinds of microwave-safe cooking utensils that we use in each recipe. Most of them are containers which can be purchased at your local grocery store, such as tempered glass pie, cake or casserole dishes. Microwave-safe plastic trays or plates are also handy for cooking as well as serving.

We cover most appetizers with waxed paper during microwaving; we feel this method results in even cooking. Remember that food continues to cook after it is removed from the microwave. To prevent over cooking, microwave food just until the last suggested microwave time in each recipe; let stand, then if not done to your liking microwave at 30 second intervals.

Stuffed Mushrooms Supreme

Sun-dried tomatoes provide a tart, chewy flavor; fresh tomatoes would result in a different product.

15 to 20 medium mushrooms (about 3/4 lb.)
1 tablespoon finely chopped ripe olives,
  drained
2 tablespoons finely chopped sun-dried
  tomatoes, packed in oil, drained,
  patted dry with paper towels

2 tablespoons goat cheese
1/8 teaspoon seasoned pepper
2 teaspoons chopped fresh basil or 1/2 teaspoon
  dried basil leaves
1/8 teaspoon salt
1 teaspoon chopped fresh chives

Wipe mushrooms with a damp cloth; remove and finely chop stems. In small bowl, combine chopped stems, olives, tomatoes, goat cheese, seasoned pepper, basil, salt and chives. Spoon into mushroom caps. Arrange, in a circle, on a 10-inch round microwave-safe dish. If you have more mushrooms than will fit in a circle, place them in concentric circles. Cover with waxed paper; microwave on 100% (HIGH) 2 minutes. Rotate dish 1/4 turn. Exchange mushrooms on inside of dish with those on outside. Microwave on 100% (HIGH) 1 minute or until heated through. Makes 15 to 20 appetizer servings.

Three Way Gnocchi

Do not use a food processor to mash potatoes; the result is a gummy mixture.

3 medium baking potatoes (5 to 6 oz. each)
1/4 teaspoon salt
2 to 3 tablespoons all-purpose flour
3 tablespoons melted butter
2 tablespoons chopped fresh chives
1 teaspoon finely chopped cilantro
1 jalapeno pepper, minced
1 tablespoon minced sun-dried tomatoes,
  packed in oil, drained, patted dry
  with paper towels

1 teaspoon minced fresh basil or
  1/4 teaspoon dried basil leaves
1 tablespoon finely chopped ripe olives,
  drained
1 tablespoon crumbled goat cheese
1/4 cup grated Parmesan cheese (1 oz.)

Prick potatoes several times with a fork. Line bottom of microwave oven with a paper towel. Arrange potatoes, to form a triangle, on paper towel. Microwave on 100% (HIGH) for 3-1/2 minutes. Turn potatoes over. Microwave on 100% (HIGH) 3 to 4 minutes or until potatoes give slightly when squeezed. Wrap in a towel; let stand 2 minutes. When cool enough to handle, peel; mash potato meat with potato masher or electric mixer. Gradually stir in salt and enough flour to make dough smooth and pliable. Divide potato mixture into pieces about the size of an egg. Shape each piece into a 1/2-inch thick 12-inch long log. Cut logs into 1-inch lengths; set aside. Brush bottom of a 12-inch round microwave-safe plate with 1/2 tablespoon of the melted butter. Arrange pieces, in a single layer, about 1/4-inch apart, in concentric circles on prepared plate. Brush gnocchi with the remaining 2-1/2 tablespoons melted butter. Microwave uncovered on 100% (HIGH) 6-1/2 minutes, rotating plate 1/4 turn after 3 minutes. Sprinkle chives, cilantro and jalapeno pepper in a wedge shape over 1/3 of gnocchi; sprinkle tomatoes and basil in a wedge shape over another 1/3. Top remaining 1/3 of gnocchi with olives and goat cheese. Sprinkle Parmesan cheese over all. Microwave uncovered on 100% (HIGH) for 1 minute or until warmed through. Use wooden picks to spear morsels. Makes about 72 appetizer servings.

Spanish Potato Onion Tapas

Our version of a classic tapas appetizer served in the bars of Spain.

1 link hot Italian sausage (8 or 9 oz.)
2 medium baking potatoes, peeled
  and sliced 1/8-inch thick
  (5 to 6 oz. each)
1 medium onion, thinly sliced and
  separated into rings

4 eggs, beaten slightly
1/4 teaspoon salt
1/8 teaspoon pepper
2 tablespoons sliced green onion or
  chopped green bell pepper
1 medium tomato

Remove casing from sausage. Crumble into an 8-inch round microwave-safe dish. Cover with waxed paper. Microwave at 50% (MEDIUM) for 2 minutes, stir after 1 minute (sausage will still be pink). Remove sausage to a bowl. In the 8-inch round microwave-safe dish, layer uncooked potatoes, partially cooked sausage and onion. Cover with waxed paper; microwave on 100% (HIGH) for 3 minutes; rotate dish 1/4 turn. Microwave on 100% (HIGH) 3 minutes or until potatoes are almost fork-tender. Remove dish from oven. In a medium bowl, combine eggs, salt and pepper; blend well. Pour over cooked potatoes; recover with waxed paper. Microwave on 50% (MEDIUM) for 2 minutes. Rotate dish 1/4 turn. Microwave on 100% (HIGH) 1 minute. Sprinkle with green onion or green pepper. Recover with waxed paper and let stand 2 minutes. If eggs are not set, microwave on 100% (HIGH) at 30 second intervals until done. Slice tomato; halve each slice. Garnish dish with tomato slices. To serve, cut into small wedges. Makes 12 to 15 appetizer servings.

Stuffed New Potatoes   Photo on cover.

These bite-sized potato boats hold a spicy cargo.

12 small new thin skinned potatoes
  (about 1 lb. total)
1/3 cup plain yogurt
1/4 teaspoon dried red chili pepper flakes,
  crushed

2 teaspoons chopped fresh chives
2 tablespoons minced sun-dried tomatoes,
  packed in oil, drained, patted dry on
  paper towels
Chopped fresh chives for garnish

Prick each potato at least once. Arrange in a circle, on a paper towel-lined, 10-inch shallow microwave-safe dish. Cover with waxed paper; microwave on 100% (HIGH) 3 minutes. Turn potatoes over. Microwave on 100% (HIGH) 2 to 3 minutes or until they give slightly when squeezed. Let stand, covered, while preparing filling. In a small bowl, combine yogurt, chili pepper, the 2 teaspoons chives and tomatoes. Halve potatoes; with melon baller or teaspoon, scoop out center leaving at least a 1/4-inch thick shell. Use centers for another purpose if desired. Spoon yogurt mixture into the center of cooked potatoes. Sprinkle with additional chives. Place half of potatoes, filling side up, in a circle, on a 10-inch microwave-safe dish. Recover with waxed paper; microwave on 100% (HIGH) 1 minute or until heated through. Repeat with remaining potatoes. Makes 24 appetizer servings.

Green 'n Gold Vegetable Nachos

If you enjoy hot, spicy foods, sprinkle with chopped jalapeno peppers just before serving.

2 uncooked medium green zucchini
   (3 to 4 oz. each)
2 uncooked medium yellow zucchini or
   crookneck squash (3 to 4 oz. each)
1 medium tomato, peeled, seeded and
   chopped

1/4 cup chopped green onions
1 tablespoon chopped fresh cilantro
1/2 teaspoon salt
1/8 teaspoon pepper
1 cup shredded Jarlsberg or Swiss cheese (4 oz.)

Cut zucchini into 1/4-inch-thick diagonal slanting slices. In a 12-inch round microwave-safe dish, arrange alternate circles of green and yellow squash. Cover with waxed paper. Microwave on 100% (HIGH) 3 minutes. Rotate dish 1/4 turn. Microwave on 100% (HIGH) an additional minute or until squash is almost fork-tender. Sprinkle chopped tomato, green onions, cilantro, salt, pepper and cheese over cooked squash. Microwave on 70% (MEDIUM-HIGH) 3 to 4 minutes or until cheese melts. To eat, pick up individual slices of squash. Makes 48 appetizer servings.

Eggplant Pâté

Wonderful garlic-flavored spread—you can omit the garlic, and it's still delicious!

1 medium eggplant (about 1 lb.)
2 tablespoons water
1 teaspoon Dijon-style mustard
1 tablespoon chopped fresh basil or
   1 teaspoon dried basil leaves
2 tablespoons chopped parsley
2 tablespoons plain yogurt
1 garlic clove, chopped

2 tablespoons sun-dried tomatoes,
   packed in oil, drained, patted dry
   with paper towels
1/4 teaspoon salt
1/8 teaspoon pepper
1 tablespoon olive oil
Pita bread, cut into thin wedges

Peel and dice eggplant into 1/2-inch cubes. Place eggplant in a 2-quart microwave-safe casserole dish. Stir in water. Cover with waxed paper and microwave on 100% (HIGH) for 5 minutes. Stir and microwave 4 minutes or until eggplant is fork-tender; drain thoroughly, then place in a food processor or blender. Add mustard, basil, parsley, yogurt, garlic, tomatoes, salt, pepper and olive oil. Process until almost smooth. Spoon into a small serving bowl. Cover and refrigerate at least 2 hours. Spread on wedges of pita bread. Makes about 1-1/2 cups.

Down-Under Marinated Mussels

Our favorites are the jumbo New Zealand green tipped mussels.

20 to 24 fresh mussels in shells
3/4 cup vegetable oil
1/4 cup white wine vinegar
2 tablespoons chopped green onion
1 teaspoon chopped fresh tarragon or
  1/4 teaspoon dried tarragon leaves

2 tablespoons chopped pimiento, drained
2 teaspoons chopped cilantro
1/4 teaspoon salt
1/8 teaspoon pepper
Fresh tarragon sprigs for garnish

Scrub mussels and remove beards; rinse in bowl of cold water. In a shallow 9-inch- or 10-inch microwave-safe casserole with lid, arrange half of mussels, in a circle, leaving center open, if possible. Cover and microwave on 100% (HIGH) 1 minute. Rotate dish 1/4 turn. Microwave on 100% (HIGH) 1 to 2 minutes or until shells open. Remove cooked mussels to a plate as they open, to avoid overcooking. Discard any unopened shells. Repeat with remaining mussels. When cool enough to handle, pull meat from shells; reserve meat and refrigerate half of shells. In a medium bowl, combine oil, vinegar, onion, tarragon, pimiento, cilantro, salt and pepper. Gently stir in mussel meat. Cover and chill at least 2 hours. Drain mussels; place one on each chilled half-shell. Arrange shells on a large deep ice-filled tray. Garnish with fresh tarragon sprigs. Makes 20 to 24 appetizer servings.

Sicilian Stuffed Sole

This is a mini version of a traditional main dish served throughout Sicily.

6 fillets of sole or other thin fish fillets,
  1/4-inch thick (1 lb.)
1 cup dry bread crumbs
1/4 cup toasted pine nuts, chopped
1/4 cup golden raisins, chopped
1 egg, beaten slightly

2 tablespoons orange juice
1/2 cup shredded mozzarella cheese (2 oz.)
1/2 teaspoon salt
2 tablespoons olive oil or vegetable oil
2 tablespoons grated Parmesan cheese
1/2 cup dry bread crumbs

Halve fillets to make 12 crosswise pieces. In a medium bowl, combine 1 cup dry bread crumbs, pine nuts, raisins, egg, orange juice, mozzarella cheese and salt. Place about 2 tablespoons filling in center of each piece of fish, 1/4-inch from edge. Fold each fillet piece in half to cover filling. Secure with one or two small wooden picks. Brush rolls with oil. In a shallow pan, combine Parmesan cheese and the 1/2 cup dry bread crumbs. Roll and pat cheese-crumb mixture on outside of fish rolls. Place 6 rolls at a time, in spoke fashion, on a shallow 8-inch round microwave-safe dish. Microwave, uncovered, on 100% (HIGH) for 2 minutes. Rotate each filled roll 1/2 turn. Microwave on 100% (HIGH) for 2 minutes or until fish barely flakes when prodded with a fork in thickest portion. Remove to a cutting board. Repeat with remaining 6 rolls. Cut each cooked roll, crosswise, into 3 pieces. Makes 36 appetizer servings.

How to Make Down-Under Marinated Mussles

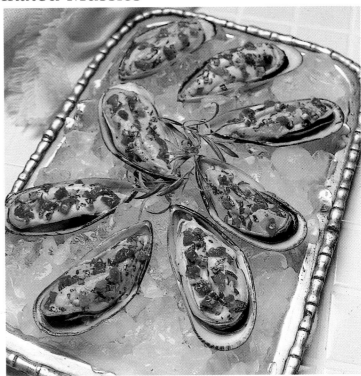

1/Scrub shells to remove grit. Cut off beards with scissors. Keep mussels on ice to prevent opening.

2/To keep marinated mussels cold, serve on a deep ice-lined tray. Garnish with fresh tarragon sprigs.

Peppered Artichoke & Salmon Spread

Serve this appetizer in its baking dish or carefully slide it onto a more decorative tray.

2 (6-oz.) jars marinated artichoke hearts, drained
2 eggs, beaten slightly
1/3 cup feta cheese, crumbled (1-1/2 oz.)
3 ounces smoked salmon (lox), chopped

1 leek washed, drained and thinly sliced
1/4 cup chopped red bell pepper
1/2 cup grated Parmesan cheese (2 oz.)
Chopped red bell pepper for garnish
Crackers or small wedges of pita bread

Grease a 9-inch round microwave-safe casserole dish; set aside. Chop artichoke hearts. Place in medium bowl with eggs, feta cheese, salmon, leek, the 1/4 cup red pepper and Parmesan cheese; combine. Pour mixture into prepared dish. Cover with waxed paper. Microwave on 70% (MEDIUM-HIGH) 5 minutes. Rotate dish 1/4 turn. Microwave on 70% (MEDIUM-HIGH) 3 minutes. Let stand, covered, 2 to 3 minutes. Garnish with a ring of chopped red peppers. Spread on crackers or pita bread wedges. Makes about 3 cups.

Treasure Island Shrimp   Photo on cover.

For a taste of the tropics, these appetizers are a winner.

**3/4 pound uncooked medium shrimp
  (about 30 to 35)**
1/2 cup all-purpose flour
1 egg, beaten slightly
1/2 teaspoon curry powder

**2 tablespoons chutney syrup (no fruit),
  see tip below**
1-1/4 cups finely chopped flaked coconut
2 tablespoons butter or margarine

Remove shells but keep tails on shrimp. Split each shrimp lengthwise, from top down, almost but not all the way through; remove sand vein. Open shrimp to resemble a butterfly shape. Place flour in a dish. In a small bowl, mix egg with curry and chutney syrup. Place coconut in a shallow dish. Dip each shrimp into flour. Dip in egg mixture; then coat with coconut. Melt 1 tablespoon butter on 100% (HIGH) in a round shallow 10-inch microwave-safe dish; brush to coat dish. Microwave half of the shrimp at a time on 100% (HIGH) for 2-1/2 minutes, let stand 1 minute. Shrimp should no longer be opaque when cut. If they need further cooking, microwave on 100% (HIGH) at 30 second intervals until done. Remove to a serving platter. Clean microwave dish. Repeat with remaining butter and shrimp. Makes 30 to 35 appetizer servings.

NOTE:
To make chutney syrup—place chutney in a strainer over a bowl. Using the back of a spoon, smash chutney against strainer to press out enough syrup to make 2 tablespoons. Return fruit chunks remaining in strainer to chutney container.

Reuben Pick-ups

Use either home-cooked corned beef or purchase it from the deli.

**7 thin slices cooked corned beef
  (about 4 ozs.)**
1 teaspoon prepared mustard

1-1/2 ounces Swiss cheese
1/3 cup sauerkraut, well drained
1-1/2 tablespoons Thousand Island dressing

Cut corned beef slices in half to make 14 strips. Thinly spread one side of each strip with mustard. Cut cheese into 14 (1'' x 1/2'' x 1/4'') pieces; place 1 on each strip of corned beef. Top with about 1 teaspoon sauerkraut and a dab of dressing. Roll up and secure with a wooden pick. Arrange, in a circle, in an 8-inch round microwave-safe dish; cover with waxed paper and microwave on 100% (HIGH) 1 minute or until cheese melts. Let stand 1 minute before serving. Makes 14 appetizer servings.

Peppered Beef Roll-Ups

Serve this beef medium rare: if overcooked to the well done stage it becomes tough.

1 lb. beef flank steak, trimmed of fat
1/4 cup olive oil or vegetable oil
1 cup dry red wine
1 garlic clove, crushed

1 teaspoon salt
1/4 teaspoon pepper
6 (7-inch) flour tortillas or pita breads,
   cut into quarters

Sour Cream Sauce:
1/2 cup dairy sour cream
1/4 cup Dijon-style mustard
2 tablespoons green peppercorns,
   drained, crushed

2 tablespoons Worcestershire sauce
2 tablespoons chopped fresh chives

Prepare Sour Cream Sauce; cover and refrigerate until needed. Partially freeze steak about 30 minutes to make it easier to slice thinly. Slice across grain, into 3/8-inch strips. In an 8'' x 4'' loaf dish combine oil, wine, garlic, salt and pepper. Add steak strips; stir to coat. Cover and refrigerate at least 4 hours or overnight; drain and discard marinade. Place half of meat strips in a 9-inch microwave-safe plate. Cover with waxed paper. Microwave on 100% (HIGH) 1-1/2 minutes. Stir once, bringing uncooked meat to outside of dish. Microwave on 100% (HIGH) for 1 minute or until done to your liking. Repeat with remaining meat. To serve, place 2 strips of steak on a tortilla wedge or pita wedge. Top with a dab of sauce. Roll up and secure with a wooden pick. Makes about 24 appetizer servings.

Sour Cream Sauce:
In a small bowl, combine all ingredients.

Sweet 'n Spicy Riblets

If you enjoy a more spicy flavor, increase the amount of red pepper flakes.

2-1/2- to 3-lbs. pork spareribs,
   cut in half crosswise
3/4 cup apricot jam
2 tablespoons orange juice

1/2 teaspoon grated orange peel
1/4 cup chunky-style peanut butter
1/4 teaspoon salt
1/4 teaspoon dried red chili pepper flakes

Cut spareribs between bones to form individual riblets; set aside. In a small bowl, combine jam, orange juice, orange peel, peanut butter, salt and red pepper flakes; set aside. Arrange ribs, back-side-up, in a shallow, 12-inch round microwave-safe dish. Cover with waxed paper; microwave on 100% (HIGH) 5 minutes. Exchange uncooked ribs on inside of dish with those on outside. Microwave 70% (MEDIUM-HIGH) 10 minutes. Drain and turn ribs. Brush with sauce. Microwave, uncovered, on 70% (MEDIUM-HIGH) 6 minutes. Let stand, covered, 5 minutes before serving. Makes 25 to 30 appetizer servings.

Pork Spirals

An impressive appetizer to serve before an Oriental dinner.

4 lean pork chops or cutlets,
about 1/2-inch thick (2 lbs.)
Salt and pepper
1 tablespoon Dijon-style mustard
12 slender green onions, trimmed
2 tablespoons honey

2 tablespoons soy sauce
2 tablespoons hoisin sauce
1 garlic clove, crushed
2 tablespoons vegetable oil
1 teaspoon sesame oil
Green onions for garnish

Remove bones from chops; trim fat. Place chops, 2 inches apart, between two sheets of plastic wrap or waxed paper. With a meat mallet, lightly pound pork to about 1/8-inch thick scallops. Sprinkle one side of each scallop with salt and pepper, then spread with mustard. Arrange 3 green onions on long end of mustard coated side of each scallop. Cut off green tops from onions to make them the same length as the piece of meat. Roll up; secure with one or two wooden picks. Place rolls in a 9-inch square microwave-safe dish. In a small bowl, combine honey, soy sauce, hoisin sauce, garlic, vegetable oil and sesame oil; pour over pork rolls. Cover and marinate at least 2 hours. Drain; reserve marinade. Arrange rolls in dish. Cover with waxed paper. Microwave on 50% (MEDIUM) for 3-1/2 minutes. Exchange uncooked rolls on inside of dish with those on outside. Microwave on 50% (MEDIUM) for 3 minutes or until no longer pink when cut. Brush with sauce. Cut each roll, crosswise, into 8 to 9 slices. Arrange on a serving plate and garnish with green onions. Makes 32 to 36 appetizer servings.

Raspberry Orange Turkey Kabobs

Purchase a turkey breast or thigh.

1/2 cup fresh or frozen unsweetened
raspberries
1/2 cup chicken broth or bouillon
1/2 cup toasted, skinned hazelnuts (2 oz.)
1/2 teaspoon salt
1/4 teaspoon pepper

1 pound uncooked turkey, boned, skinned,
cut in 1-inch cubes
1 tablespoon black raspberry liqueur
2 tablespoons dairy sour cream
2 oranges, peeled and cut into bite-size pieces

In a food processor or blender, combine raspberries, broth, hazelnuts, salt and pepper. Process until nuts are finely chopped. Arrange uncooked turkey pieces in a shallow 9-inch round microwave-safe dish. Pour raspberry mixture over turkey; stir to coat. Cover with waxed paper; microwave on 70% (MEDIUM-HIGH) for 3 minutes. Stir, recover and microwave 100% (HIGH) 2 minutes. Let stand 1 minute; meat should no longer be pink when cut. If they need further cooking, microwave on 100% (HIGH) at 30 second intervals until done. With a slotted spoon, remove turkey pieces from dish. Stir liqueur and sour cream into raspberry mixture then pour into a serving dish. Thread 1 cube of cooked poultry and 1 piece of orange on small wooden skewers and place on a serving tray. Let each guest dip kabobs into warm sauce. Makes 20 to 25 appetizer servings.

How to Make Pork Spirals

1/Remove bone; trim off fat. Pound chop with meat mallet or rolling pin to 1/8-inch thickness.

2/Pork rolls with green onion centers make easy finger food. Use green onion fans for garnish.

Chicken-Prosciutto Meatballs

For a change of pace, dip these cooked tidbits in chutney just before serving.

1 lb. uncooked chicken; skinned,
** boned and cubed**
1/4 lb. thinly sliced prosciutto, chopped
1 tablespoon chopped parsley
1/4 teaspoon grated orange peel
2 teaspoons chopped fresh chives
1 egg
1/2 cup soft breadcrumbs

1/3 cup dairy sour cream
2 teaspoons Worcestershire sauce
1/2 teaspoon salt
1/8 teaspoon pepper
3/4 cup chicken broth or bouillon
1/4 cup white wine
1 teaspoon grated fresh gingerroot
Chopped fresh chives for garnish

In a food processor, combine chicken, prosciutto, parsley, orange peel and the 2 teaspoons chives. Process until meat is ground. Add egg, breadcrumbs, sour cream, Worcestershire sauce, salt and pepper; process until well blended. Form into about 55 (1-inch) balls. Combine broth, wine, and ginger in a 10-inch round microwave-safe casserole dish. Cover with waxed paper. Microwave on 100% (HIGH) for 1 minute or until boiling. Add half the meatballs; recover with waxed paper. Microwave on 100% (HIGH) 2 minutes. Rotate dish 1/4 turn; microwave on 100% (HIGH) 30 seconds or until meatballs are no longer pink when cut. With slotted spoon, remove meatballs from liquid to a serving bowl; cover to keep warm. Repeat with remaining meatballs. Just before serving sprinkle with chives; serve warm. Makes about 55 appetizer servings.

Two-way Chicken Tidbits

A clever way to give your guests a choice of flavors.

6 boneless chicken breast halves (1-1/2 lbs.)
3 tablespoons chutney
1 tablespoon chopped green onion
2 tablespoons vegetable oil
2 tablespoons chunk-style peanut butter
1/4 teaspoon salt

1/4 teaspoon dried red chili pepper flakes
2 tablespoons soy sauce
1 tablespoon honey
2 teaspoons chopped gingerroot
1 tablespoon toasted sesame seeds
1 tablespoon vegetable oil

Remove and discard chicken skin. Cut meat into 1-1/2-inch chunks. Divide meat between 2 (9-inch) microwave-safe dishes. Cover and refrigerate while preparing sauces. In blender or food processor, combine chutney, green onion, 2 tablespoons vegetable oil, peanut butter, salt and chili peppers. Process until finely chopped but not smooth. Pour over one dish of chicken chunks; toss to coat, recover and refrigerate 30 minutes. In a blender or food processor, combine soy sauce, honey, ginger, sesame seeds and the 1 tablespoon vegetable oil. Process until almost smooth; pour over second dish of chicken; toss to coat, recover and refrigerate 30 minutes. Cover with waxed paper and microwave each dish separately on 70% (MEDIUM-HIGH) for 2-1/2 minutes. Stir, recover, and microwave on 70% (MEDIUM-HIGH) 1 to 1-1/2 minutes. Let stand, covered, 1 minute. Chicken should no longer be pink when cut. If they need further cooking, microwave on 70% (MEDIUM-HIGH) at 30 second intervals until done to your liking. Makes 40 to 45 appetizer servings.

Metric Chart
Comparison to Metric Measure

When You Know	Symbol	Multiply By	To Find	Symbol
teaspoons	tsp	5.0	milliliters	ml
tablespoons	tbsp	15.0	milliliters	ml
fluid ounces	fl. oz.	30.0	milliliters	ml
cups	c	0.24	liters	l
pints	pt.	0.47	liters	l
quarts	qt.	0.95	liters	l
ounces	oz.	28.0	grams	g
pounds	lb.	0.45	kilograms	kg
Fahrenheit	F	5/9 (after subtracting 32)	Celsius	C

Liquid Measure to Milliliters

1/4 teaspoon	=	1.25 milliliters
1/2 teaspoon	=	2.5 milliliters
3/4 teaspoon	=	3.75 milliliters
1 teaspoon	=	5.0 milliliters
1-1/4 teaspoons	=	6.25 milliliters
1-1/2 teaspoons	=	7.5 milliliters
1-3/4 teaspoons	=	8.75 milliliters
2 teaspoons	=	10.0 milliliters
1 tablespoon	=	15.0 milliliters
2 tablespoons	=	30.0 milliliters

Liquid Measure to Liters

1/4 cup	=	0.06 liters
1/2 cup	=	0.12 liters
3/4 cup	=	0.18 liters
1 cup	=	0.24 liters
1-1/4 cups	=	0.3 liters
1-1/2 cups	=	0.36 liters
2 cups	=	0.48 liters
2-1/2 cups	=	0.6 liters
3 cups	=	0.72 liters
3-1/2 cups	=	0.84 liters
4 cups	=	0.96 liters
4-1/2 cups	=	1.08 liters
5 cups	=	1.2 liters
5-1/2 cups	=	1.32 liters

Index

Index

Index